TEACHING,
LEARNING,
LITERACY
in Our
HIGH-RISK
HIGH-TECH World

TEACHING, LEARNING, LITERACY in Our HIGH-RISK HIGH-TECH World

A Framework for Becoming Human

James Paul Gee

TEACHERS COLLEGE PRESS

TEACHERS COLLEGE | COLUMBIA UNIVERSITY
NEW YORK AND LONDON

Published by Teachers College Press, 1234 Amsterdam Avenue, New York, NY
10027

Copyright © 2017 by Teachers College, Columbia University

Cover photos credits: Game controller by crossstudio/iStock by Getty Images;
Students looking at laptop by Creative-Family/iStock by Getty Images; Baby by
Inara Prusakova/Shutterstock; Bacteria by royaltystockphoto/Shutterstock.

Library of Congress Cataloging-in-Publication Data is available at loc.gov

ISBN 978-0-8077-5860-1 (paper)
ISBN 978-0-8077-7595-0 (ebook)

Printed on acid-free paper
Manufactured in the United States of America

24 23 22 21 20 19 18 17   8 7 6 5 4 3 2 1

Contents

CHAPTER 1

Introduction
Leaping Across the Silos

This is a book about learning, language, and literacy. It's also about brains and bodies. And it's about talk, texts, media, and society. These topics are usually studied in different narrow academic silos. Yet they are all part of one interactive process: the process of human development (Center for the Developing Child at Harvard University, 2016). If we move across all the relevant silos, rather than diving deeply into only one, we can gain a bigger picture of how children and adults learn and develop.

Here is a snapshot of the big picture this book will develop, of the forces and processes that influence learning and development, and of needed adjustments in a new age:

Design (BEING) →
Experience (DOING) →
Mentoring →
Memory →
Sense-Making/Future Planning/Pattern Recognition
　(KNOWING) → Talk/Texts/Media →
Generalizations →
Affinity (Motivation, interest, maybe even passion
　grows) → (BECOMING)
Self-Teaching →
Identities (BEING)

In sum, people who *are* something (parents, teachers, gamers, cooks, gardeners, physicists, etc.) design motivating environments in which children and newbies (adults new to an area) have experiences that lead to good learning. Such experiences involve learners DOING things, taking actions whose outcomes they really care about.

In these designed experiences, children and newbies get help from mentors and teachers to know what to pay attention to and how best to store a useful memory of the experience in long-term memory. In turn, children and newbies use these memories to make sense of things going on around them, to prepare for future action, and to find patterns and subpatterns across their experiences that eventually constitute general knowledge, that is, KNOWING.

Children and newbies need lots of talk with adults or more advanced peers about how to think about experience and how to test patterns for accuracy, if generalization is to work well. They also need critical capacities to use texts and media of all sorts to engage in drawing accurate and useful generalizations from experience and evidence.

As part of this whole ongoing process—and via their trusting collaborations with teachers and mentors—children and newbies, over time, build up motivation, interest, and maybe even passion for certain forms of knowledge, ways of producing that knowledge, and values that they can eventually share with others with similar commitments in the world. They gain an affinity for something that can lead to affiliations with other people and their goals and values. They are preparing to BECOME something.

As these processes of development unfold, children and newbies become (we hope) deliberate learners who know how to teach and mentor themselves and how to design good learning environments for themselves. At this point they have BECOME, for example, members of a family or community, committed students, gardeners, citizens, gamers, teachers, citizen scientists, biologists, activists, and so on, through many possibilities.

We often think of learning and development as happening inside our brains and bodies, but we humans have a very inaccurate view of what our brains and bodies—and, indeed, our very selves—really are and do. The brain is crucial to learning, of course. But a person actually has two brains, not one: One brain is in our head and another is in our gut, and the gut brain communicates to the head brain and strongly influences our mental health and how we feel, think, and behave (McAuliffe, 2016; Yong, 2016).

Science is just getting started on studying the brain and the body at this level. Much remains to be discovered, and important new results are coming fast and furious. Recently the neurosurgeon James Doty (2016) argued that we have a third brain, the heart. We think of our head brain as making free decisions for which we are responsible. But the vast majority of the brain is composed of modules (subsystems) that make decisions about how we feel, think, believe, and behave in ways that are inaccessible to our conscious awareness. The conscious part of our brain largely plays catch-up, by trying to make up good stories about why we feel, believe, and behave as we do, especially when the conscious brain does not know the relevant processes of the rest of the brain that lead us to think, behave, or feel as we do (Gazzaniga, 1988, 2011). The understanding that it is often our gut that is doing the thinking makes it more important than ever that we become reflective thinkers and also test our thinking in collaboration with others.

We think of memory as providing an accurate record of the past. But in reality human memory is as much about the future as it is about the past, or more so (Marcus, 2008; Renfrew, 2009). We use our memories to make sense of things, prepare for future actions, and create stories about ourselves and our lives. As we do these things, we change our memories in ways based on the uses we have made of them. Thus, human memory changes over time and is not very good at factual accuracy about the past (Loftus, 1976).

Learning and development require a head brain and a gut brain; they require a body. They also require a society. Learning and development—a person's knowing things, being able to do things, having an identity—are all reciprocal and interacting processes among brains; bodies; environments; other people; and the social, cultural, and institutional groups into which people fall.

Humans learn from experience. You have to have a body to have an experience. And for most experiences you have to have social interactions with other people. Though researchers often use computers to model human learning, computers do not have bodies and so cannot have experiences. A computer at a restaurant might correctly pair the right wine with one's favorite dish, but it will never know how that food tastes and feels on the palate. And computers cannot have social interactions. A computer can have a "conversation" with a human, but it will never know or feel the heft, the warp and weave, of human needs, fears, hopes, and desires. Thus, computers cannot and do not learn and develop in the way humans do.

What develops is not just an organism, an individual, a child, but an immensely complex system. Research on interacting brains, bodies, and environments has long concluded that each of us is as complex as the universe, indeed probably more so (Marcus & Freeman,

2015; Swaab, 2014). This is why narrow silos can be dangerous when we deal with learning and development. Wrong ideas here can do real harm.

Learning and development today take place in a different world from that of the past. Humans across the globe face serious risks, dangers, and disasters from interacting complex systems that are on the verge of going out of control. These are systems like massive inequality, environmental degradation, global warming, vast migration flows, a global economy based on streams of numbers in computers, religious and cultural conflicts, the loss of many jobs, and the transformation of work as a result of new technologies.

Our world today is so complicated—and human individual intelligence so frail—that we all need to learn how to engage in collective intelligence. Collective intelligence means networking together diverse people and smart tools in the right ways to solve hard problems beyond the grasp of any one person, skill, or method (Nielsen, 2012).

Research on collective intelligence has amply demonstrated that in order to function well, smart groups need to be diverse (Brown & Lauder, 2000; Leimeister, 2010; Surowiecki, 2004). However, the big categories that we usually think represent diversity—race, class, gender, and ability—sometimes do more to efface diversity than to capture it. For collective intelligence, the diversity that counts is the different ways different people have worked out to be things like Asian Americans, women, members of the working class, or individuals with a learning disability, given their specific experiences and contexts in life.

Narrow specializations in narrow academic silos have brought us a great deal of progress in science. But times are changing. When we face highly complex problems, narrow expertise can become dangerous. Narrow experts tend to underestimate and undervalue what they don't know (Harford, 2011; Jenkins, 2006; Weinberger, 2012). They tend to think that their methods answer complex questions that, in reality, go well beyond their area of expertise. And they tend to engage in "groupthink" as they converge in their narrow echo chambers, advancing paradigms that are not tested against the results of other silos.

We are all aware that, thanks to digital technologies, opportunities for learning have become ubiquitous outside school. What fewer people realize is that teaching has also become ubiquitous outside school. Some people are using the Internet and other electronic means to become uncredentialed experts (and not just self-proclaimed experts, but fraudulent ones, of which there are many too, of course) (Anderson, 2012; Hitt, 2013). They work together to produce knowledge, citizen science, media, products, and inventions that rival what credentialed experts can do, certainly what they can do alone. But they also organize themselves into what I call *affinity spaces*, places where teaching of all different sorts goes on (Gee, 2013; Gee & Hayes, 2010).

When we talk about learning and development today we have to put school into the larger context of diverse teaching and learning practices, diverse literacy and media practices, and diverse things to know and be, in and out of school. Isolating school from teaching and learning out of school will harm children and lead to even greater inequality of opportunity and results.

Regardless of how we think about traditional narrow experts and their silos, thinking in terms of only one silo will not do for parents, teachers, or policymakers. Development does not happen in silos and does not separate the many topics we are trying to integrate in this book. The information parents, teachers, and policymakers must draw on, and even help us discover, resides in no one single silo or even in just a few. And, of course, not all we need to know is academic in any narrow sense.

Generalizing, in order to view the big picture, can be dangerous, of course. It is easy to overlook important details in the gold mines of knowledge that constitute our academic silos. It is easy to be wrong, though thankfully being wrong is often a good thing (Gee, 2013; Harford, 2011). However, *ignoring* the big picture is much more dangerous. Seeking to help and provide resources to people with but one tool or remedy is often shortsighted and harmful. It is particularly dangerous today when many of the problems we all face are multifaceted and complex.

A problem every parent and teacher confronts is how to help children develop into healthy, flourishing humans in a very complex and high-risk world. Furthermore, how can they continue to develop and flourish in a world where drastic change will be the norm? These are hard problems. The answers require connecting, integrating, and finding synergies among all the topics we will deal with in this book.

The claims in this book are not meant to be taken at face value as undeniably true. I hope they are true, but if they are not I want us to come together to identify where they need work and how we can improve them. *My* goal is to be as clear as I can about my perspective on learning and development so that you, the reader, can reflect on your own. Perhaps, in the process, you may learn more about your own perspective; possibly deepen it; and, if you feel the need, change or transform it by contrasting and comparing it with mine and with others'. That is my goal for myself as well. The goal of my writing is not conversion, but mutual mulling.

In a world where a great many people are profoundly harmed by injustice, hatred, and fear, I do not know the exact right place to go to make things better. All I have are some suggestions about the journey we might take together. And I have a fervent hope that we will find good places to go together on a journey that may nonetheless never reach a final resting place. The journey itself is our hope.

Just as this book attempts to escape narrow academic silos, it also seeks to address a wide range of readers. I want to address teachers and parents, activists young and old, policymakers, and academics from various fields; my goal is to reach those who care about learning and development in the contemporary world.

In the book, I use a number of examples that are drawn from my own life and experiences. I do so for two reasons: First, I want to avoid talking about other people's lived realities, especially people who may not see me as sufficiently like them to give me the right to speak about them. Second, I want to encourage all my readers, who-ever they are, to see their own unique lived experiences as sources of crucial information for how we might save ourselves together, before we all perish alone, each in his or her own separate capsizing boats, on a violent sea.

CHAPTER 2

Experiences and Perspectives

COMPUTERS AND PEOPLE

Digital computers and human minds are quite different things. All computers are good at things like logical reasoning and keeping financial records straight. Many humans are not.

Computers never forget, and their memories can remain unchanged forever. If their data were accurate to begin with, they remain that way as long as no one copies over them. However, humans forget things all the time. Furthermore, the accuracy of human memory is so poor that years of research have demonstrated that eyewitness testimony is unreliable (Loftus & Ketcham, 1991; Schacter, 2002).

A computer has primarily two things in it: rules and pieces of information ("facts"). It uses the rules to manipulate the information. For example, a computer could be programmed with the following rule set:

1. a is X
2. Every X is Y
3. Therefore, a is Y
    "a" is a name (e.g., *Fido*)
    "X" is a property (e.g., being *small*, being *a small thing*, being *a dog*)
    "Y" is a different property

When you plug words into this schema, it will lead to an infinite number of logically valid arguments of the form:

1. Socrates is a human.
2. Every human is mortal.
3. Therefore Socrates is mortal.

1. Fido is a dog.
2. Every dog is a canine.
3. Therefore Fido is a canine.

1. Glib is a glub.
2. Every glub is a gloom.
3. Thus, Glib is a gloom.

1. Gary is a mouse.
2. All mice are small.
3. Therefore Gary is small.

The computer has no idea what any of these words actually means. It is a bit like a cloze test. It as if the computer were programmed with empty slots (marked by symbols) where words can be inserted. When you insert words you get a valid argument (remember that *valid* does not necessarily mean "true").

It might sometimes seem that computers know what words mean, but they never do. Computers can be programmed with words matched to "definitions" (a string of other words) and can substitute one for the other. So in a sentence like "Herman is a bachelor" the computer can replace the word "bachelor" with the string of words "an unmarried man" and rewrite the sentence as "Herman is an unmarried man."

If you ask the computer whether the Pope is a bachelor, it will immediately say yes, since its database contains the fact "The Pope is always an unmarried man." If you ask humans, they will mull it over, and some will say no and others just really won't know what to say.

For human beings, word meanings are not just definitions. Word meaning is not just a string of other words. Word meaning, for humans, is always adjusted to context and is often a matter of negotiation (Gee, 2014, 2015a). The Pope is not in the marriage market, so is he really a bachelor? And what does *marriage* mean anyway? Does it mean "a legal status"? If so, then it can change (as it has with the U.S. Supreme Court's ruling on gay marriage). Does it mean "a bond between only a man and a woman"? What about a trans man? Well, what does *man* really mean? Is it God, or courts, or everyday people that determine what words mean?

EXPERIENCES: WHAT HUMANS HAVE AND COMPUTERS DON'T

One very important thing is that inside human minds, but never in a computer, are memories of past experiences. Computers cannot have experiences. To have an experience you have to have a body and move around the world (Damasio, 1995, 1999) or be able to imagine being able to do so because as a human you know, through sensation, how it feels to be a human mind/body in contact with the world and others in it. Other creatures—most strikingly octopuses—have different bodies and, thus, different ways of sensing and categorizing the world (see Godfrey-Smith, 2016).

For humans, long-term memory is a storage house of past experiences. Computer memory is not. As we said, computers cannot have experiences and so they cannot store them in their memories.

It is odd that for decades, from the late 1950s to at least the 1980s, in their research, psychologists used digital computers as a model of how the human mind works. It is a bad model (Clark, 1989, 1997; Gee, 2013, 2015a). Even today, while most researchers in this field are aware that human minds are not much like digital computers, they still treat the mind primarily as an information-processing device. In reality, the human brain and body combined are an experience-processing device.

We humans, academics and nonacademics alike, cannot really say in words what an experience is. Trying to do so is as bad as to trying to describe in words how to tie one's shoes. We certainly know what an experience is when we have one, but we do not know how to say what an experience is.

We can surely float in a sea of sensation and tune out all conscious thought (as much as we can) and this is, of course, an experience. But what we might call mindful or focused experiences have at least the following properties:

1. **Sensation:** We take in (*sense*) images, sounds, smells, feelings, and sometimes words.
2. **Cognition:** We form interpretations of what we take in at many levels.
3. **Emotions:** Emotions are triggered in us that "color" what we are taking in.
4. **Attention:** We pay attention to only some aspects of an experience, since experiences are filled with far too many details for us to pay attention to all of them.
5. **Appreciation:** We appreciate, value, or evaluate what we are taking in, in certain ways.

Humans do not generally learn by initially storing generalizations and facts in their minds. They learn by having experiences in the world, storing these in the mind, and then using this database (as it gets bigger and bigger) to find patterns and subpatterns across their experiences (Clark, 1997; diSessa, 2000; Gee, 2015a; Glenberg & Gallese, 2012). These patterns and subpatterns eventually come to establish what is a "fact" in the sense of being true (thanks to evidence) and also come to establish larger generalizations.

We humans most often think and learn bottom-up, moving from concrete experiences to generalizations that we draw based on patterns we have discovered in our experiences. This process takes time and requires lots of different experiences. The generalizations we draw are composed of myriad concrete experiences (examples). Unfortunately, schools most often go the other way, starting with generalizations and then sometimes moving to a quite limited number of concrete experiences that exemplify the generalizations.

Since computers cannot have experiences, they cannot learn in the human way. They start with facts and generalizations as strings of symbols they cannot understand. We humans do not usually start with facts or generalizations; we start with embodied experiences. In turn, these embodied experiences give deep meaning to the facts and generalizations we eventually derive from them or learn from others.

LEARNING FROM EXPERIENCE

The claim *Humans learn from experience* is at the heart of this book. Yet, as it stands, it is a trivial claim. For a human being, every waking (and dreaming) moment is an experience. Thus, any learning must have been associated with some experience or other.

Furthermore, it is obvious that people can have experiences in which they learn nothing or next to nothing. If you dash across a busy road and get hit by a car and die, you have learned nothing from the experience. Even short of death, many experiences bring little illumination, and sometimes they teach us unfortunate things. For example, much social media today (along with other cultural factors) has taught too many young girls that what matters most is whether they are "hot" or "not." Such media has taught too many young boys to view girls as "achievements" in a game that has nothing to do with romance or love (Orenstein, 2016; Sales, 2016)

Yet it is true that the most primordial and fundamental form of human learning is learning from experience. But not any old experience.

The experiences that are best for learning are what I called *mindful* or *focused* experiences above. Within these sorts of experiences there are three features that are crucial for deep and long-term learning (Barsalou, 1999a, 1999b; Gee, 2013; Glenberg, 1997; Glenberg & Gallese, 2012; Lavie & Dalton, 2013; Wason, 1968). The features are:

1. The learner has an **action** to take in the experience.
2. The learner emotionally **cares** about the outcome of the action in the sense that something meaningful is at stake for the person in the outcome of the action.
3. Something or someone helps the learner to know what things in the experience are most relevant and important to pay **attention** to in order to carry out the action successfully. Any real-world experience has a great many things in it that we could pay attention to, not all of which are equally relevant or important.

So to learn well we need action, caring, and well-managed attention. At this point we are focusing on embodied experiences in the world, the primordial form of experience for human beings. Later we will see that texts and other forms of media can be sources of vicarious experience for us humans, thanks to our imaginations.

We acknowledged earlier that people can learn bad things from an experience, not just good things. So for young learners, someone has to help them make good choices about which experiences to seek out. As parents, teachers, and adults we cannot evade, in a haze of relativism, making decisions about what is good or bad for children who are too young to make such choices fully for themselves. We can debate these choices, and we can learn better choices through critical discussions with others, but we have to act, at home and in school.

WHY ACTION, CARING, AND ATTENTION ARE IMPORTANT

Why are action, caring, and attention important for successful learning from experience? The reason is that these three things are all important for how we store an experience in long-term memory (LTM). We will see later that how we store an experience in LTM determines how effective the experience is for learning, development, and our well-being.

It is important to note here that LTM in humans is as much about the future as it is about the past (more about this in the next chapter). We use the memories in our LTM not just to recall the past but also as a database for imagination and preparation for future actions and choices (Gazzaniga, 2011; Glenberg, 1997; Klein, Robertson, & Delton, 2010, 2011; Loftus, 1976; Marcus, 2008; Schacter, 2002; Swaab, 2014).

Why must we have an *action* to take? When we have an action to take, we bring goals and expectations to an experience (Glenberg, 1997). Goals and expectations help us to organize the experience at the time we are having it. They give the experience structure, much like a plot in a story or headings in an article. Thanks to this structure, they also help us to store the experience in LTM in a well-organized, coherent, and meaningful form so that the experience is well-integrated with our other stored experiences. In turn, as we will see, this makes the memory much more useful in the future.

Why is *caring* important? Lots of research has shown that when you place people in experiences where they have an action to take whose outcome they really care about and then test them later about what they have learned, they appear very smart (Cosmides, 1989; Wason, 1966, 1968). When you place them in experiences where this is not the case, they often appear stupid.

For example, it used to be thought that young children could not "conserve" quantities (Piaget, 1965). In other words, young children supposedly could not tell that a line of 10 marbles placed close together had the same number of marbles in it as a line of 10 marbles placed further apart (the latter looks longer and so seems to have more items in it), even if you moved the marbles in front of them. However, children *can* do just this if you use M&Ms instead of marbles and they want to be sure they get their fair share (Mehler & Bever, 1967; Rose & Blank, 1974).

Other research has shown that humans, both children and adults, are quite adept at logic and reasoning when things like cheating and fairness are at stake, but not nearly as adept when nothing very concrete and emotively meaningful is at stake for them. Indeed, it has been argued that in evolution, the growth of human intelligence was driven by a socially shared concern for fairness and catching cheaters (Cosmides, 1989; Cosmides, Barrett, & Tooby, 2010; Wason, 1966, 1968).

There can be all sorts of reasons why a person cares about the outcome of an action, all sorts of reasons why the person feels something is personally at stake for him or her in the outcome of the action. When humans care in this way, they process elements of an experience both cognitively (through their reasoning faculties) and emotionally (through the parts of their brain where feeling is involved in information). Research has shown that such dual-processed experiences are stored in LTM in a way that is deeper, better organized, and better integrated with other knowledge (Erk et al., 2003; Gray, Braver, & Raichle, 2002; McGaugh, Cahill, & Roozendaal, 1996; Richards & Gross, 2000). This makes these memories much better fodder for future use as well.

Why do we need help managing our *attention*? Well, we don't always. People who have become adept at some domain of knowledge or skill have learned to manage their own attention. They process and store their experiences in this domain in a fruitful fashion.

But children and adults new to a domain need help. In any experience, there are too many possible things to pay attention to. Attention is a quite limited resource for human beings (we will see later that LTM is not). If attention is not allotted to the right stuff in an effective way, we can become overwhelmed by an experience, fail to accomplish our goals, learn the wrong thing or nothing, and store the memory in a misleading or useless form or not at all (Barsalou, 2009; Gee, 2004; Lavie & Dalton, 2013). Someone (a parent, mentor, or teacher) or something (a good tool or technology) must help children and newbies manage their attentional economy well in experiences meant for learning.

None of this is to say that we humans cannot enjoy experiences where we just float in a sea of sensations. Such experiences can be a source of joy and aesthetic pleasure, even of flashes of insight (and sometimes nonsense). However, they are not the sorts of experiences that produce an education in the broad sense of producing a person who can act in the world for success, problem solving, and peace.

I am all for sometimes letting ourselves go, but learning is often about reining ourselves in, that is, focusing on certain things and not others. And, furthermore, people who have stored lots of rich, diverse, and well-integrated experiences in their LTM are the ones most open to real insights when they swim in the sea of sensation and free association.

+EXPERIENCES

I will call experiences that have the three features discussed above—action, caring, and well-managed attention—"+experiences." And I will modify the bare claim that humans learn from experience to this version:

> Most deep human learning is rooted (is founded, originates) in +experiences

This claim is simple (though often ignored in schools), but it has many important consequences. It is one of the two major claims this book will make.

Research has long shown that people can think, problem-solve, and plan better for future action if their recollections (of experience) in long-term memory are well organized, well integrated, and well connected (Barsalou, 1999a; Eichenbaum, 2008; Ericsson & Kintsch, 1995). This helps facilitate the search for useful patterns and subpatterns, the formation of useful generalizations, and the search for evidence for what to believe and act on.

As humans form generalizations on the basis of experience, they also form theories or perspectives on things. These theories or perspectives—some consciously known, some not—direct their attention and actions in the world (Gazzaniga, 1988; Holland, Lachicotte, Skinner, & Cain, 1998; Popper, 1994; Strauss & Quinn, 1997). What I am calling *perspectives* here are networks of connected claims and generalizations that form a person's expectations, beliefs, values, and actions in a given area of experience.

We all have perspectives—and different people, social groups, and cultures have different ones—on a good many things, things such as parenting, friendship, being a citizen, marriage, teaching, being a man or a woman, cooking, music, romance, and what it means to "work for a living." We deeply cherish some perspectives, especially those we have learned in our early socialization within a family and community, through co-participation in a religion, or as insiders in various sorts of groups, cultures, and institutions.

For all the deep meaning such cherished perspectives can give our lives, they can and have led to a great deal of harm and even violence in the world. Indeed, today we face a great many conflicts based on unbending ideological, cultural, and religious differences. This raises a profound issue of how we can live in peace together in an ever more divisive and polarized country and world.

In my view, for human beings to be healthy in mind and body, they need to develop and continually enlarge their capacities for testing their perspectives (Gee, 2013). They can do this by acting in and on the world and then paying respectful attention to the world's responses to ("evidence" of) their actions. And they can do it through respectful dialogue with others who have different perspectives. Sadly, though, today we are short on people committed to evidence and respectful dialogue across differences.

I will argue in this book that a key goal of schooling and human development is the creation of people who are **committed testers,** people who respect evidence, seek ways to falsify their own beliefs, and engage in civil critical discussions with others who not share their beliefs or values. I will offer ideas about how such people can cherish their core beliefs and values and nonetheless engage in meaningful critical discussion with others in a joint search for truth and peace.

All humans have a deep need to feel that what they do counts and matters to others and to society, hopefully in the service of peace and a better world for all. Education owes each child the skills necessary for effective action in the world.

At the same time, however, society must treat everyone as worthy of full and active participation. One of the greatest evils any society can inflict is to make people or whole classes of people feel they do not matter (Marmot, 2004; Pickett & Wilkinson, 2011). It leads to poor physical and mental health. It hampers learning and leads to poor development. Unfortunately, currently in the United States, and in many other countries, there are very high levels of inequality. High inequality leads far too many people to feel left out. It leads, as well, to very poor health statistics, because when people feel that what they think and do really doesn't matter, they can suffer negative health effects (Pickett & Wilkinson, 2011).

I should note that I will unashamedly use the word *truth* in this book. I will say that people need to be *truth seekers* and *truth testers.* What I mean by *truth* is not any form of final knowledge. I mean a journey (process) toward healthier, more moral, more humane, more effective, and more peaceful perspectives on the world. Such perspectives are based on respect for the world's responses when we act in it or experiment on it. They are based, as well, on respect for others when we have critical dialogues with them about what we each be-lieve we have learned from our differing experiences in the world. In almost all cases, we humans cannot attain perfection; but in almost all cases we can do better. Given the state of health, equality, and peace in the world today, the bar isn't very high.

In light of the importance of being clear about our perspectives, I want to be as accurate as I can in this book on my perspective on expe-rience and learning. This is not just because I hope I am right. It is also because I believe that if we are all clear with one another we can, in critical discussions, compare and contrast our beliefs and experiences and, in the process, get closer to truth and peace.

This idea about the importance of comparing, contrasting, and connecting perspectives—an idea essentially about communication—is the second key claim of this book:

> However close we frail human beings can ever come, over the
> long haul, to truth and peace is contingent on our being able
> to engage in critical discussions where we compare, contrast,
> connect, and debate different perspectives (what I will later call
> *frameworks*) on important issues and problems, and perhaps adapt
> and change some of our own.

The two claims I have laid out in this chapter—one about expe-riences (+experiences) and one about perspectives (directly above)—will turn out to be deeply connected. Together they lead to a variety of other claims, based in a variety of different research areas. These claims constitute a new perspective on learning, development, and what it means to be human.

I do not claim that my perspective is correct in all respects. But I do hope it can give rise to new and deeper critical discussions about learn-ing, schools, policy, society, and the modern world. We badly need, in my view, to break out of our routine assumptions in all these areas.

IS IT PRACTICAL?

Some readers will wonder whether the two key points I am making here—and will develop throughout the book—are practical. I concede that their practicality depends on what you see as the end goal of human development, learning, and education. The goal I advocate is this: Early development and lifelong education ought to prepare each and every one of us to be the following:

1. **Resilient:** Sustainability used to be a major goal for many people and institutions. Sustainability meant being able to retain core goals and values in the face of change. However, today, change is more rapid, risky, and unpredictable than ever before. So people, families, and institutions will need to be resilient (Zolli & Healy, 2012). To be resilient means being able not only to adapt to change but also, when necessary, to change, even in large ways, in the face of change, to become new. Resilient people put in lots of effort and can persist past failure and even serious setbacks, all the while accepting that humans are frail and hope is not always easy.

2. **A proactive agent:** To be a proactive agent means being able to participate (not just spectate) and produce (not just consume) in ways that matter positively for one's self, others, and our shared world. Participating and producing requires one to think like, and sometimes be, a designer of things, texts, media, or ideas.

3. **A deliberate learner:** To be a deliberate learner is to be a self-teacher, a person who can direct his or her own learning and attention and who regularly seeks out new experiences and challenges to deepen old capacities and develop new ones.

4. **Insightful:** By *insightful* I mean being able to deal with complexity and to understand systems and not just their components. I mean, as well, being able to engage fruitfully in discussion and reflection with one's self and others on multiple perspectives in the service of a slow journey to more truth and peace. These are both crucial because system complexity and conflicting perspectives are at the heart of our major problems and crises today. The goal is not consensus or conversion, but gradual progress to deeper understandings of our own perspectives and those of others.

5. **A good chooser:** Good choosers are able to make good decisions in important domains in life and recover from bad ones. They are able, as well, to seek out and find good sources of mentoring, guidance, and help. They don't just have knowledge; they use it.

None of these—certainly not all of them together—appear to be the goal of our current educational system, or of our society. What we test these days in school does not test these goals.

If, however, the preceding goals are your goals—for your child, your students, yourself—then the ideas in this book are practical. They are practical because they form the basis of how to achieve these goals and they underwrite the sorts of practices that can accomplish these goals.

Let us call people—children or adults—who are on a path to develop, at ever deeper levels, the five features named above "resilient+" people. The symbol + just stands for the other four features. Such people come to see life as a set of challenge-based quests, often requiring cooperation and collaboration with others, to achieve better (safer, more peaceful, more joyous, and fairer) selves, others, societies, institutions, and world.

The amount and diversity of +experiences a person has had, starting early in life, and the person's capacity to be a committed tester are the foundation for becoming a resilient+ person—not a victim of society and its institutions, but an agent for improving both. The development of resilient+ people is not, however, the foundation for success in many of our current schools and institutions. Too many schools and institutions today fail to nurture the features described above and sometimes even actively work—intentionally or not—to suppress them.

I should note, too, in order to forestall possible misunderstandings, that when I talk about success, proactivity, participation, and production, I do not mean that people have to have a "good job" or make a lot of money. As we will see later, many people today are finding a vital sense of counting and mattering to one another as valued knowers and doers outside markets and formal institutions.

You may well still find my ideas impractical, since "it will never happen," you might well say. Our societies and institutions may well never willingly free all people to be proactive agents and questers. History has never seen such a thing.

True, but it's a journey, not necessarily a destination that will ever be reached once and for all. It's a quest. However, we will never know if the destination is reachable unless we start and continue on the journey. Let the great Raymond Williams have the last word here:

It is only in a shared belief and insistence that there are practical alternatives that the balance of forces and chances begins to alter. Once the inevitabilities are challenged, we begin gathering our resources for a journey of hope. If there are no easy answers there are still available discoverable hard answers, and it is these that we can now learn to make and share. This has been, from the beginning, the sense and the impulse of the long revolution. (Williams, 1983, pp. 268–269)

CHAPTER 3

Memory and Imagination

MEMORY

In the way in which we normally think of memory, we do not actually have it (Gee, 2013; Glenberg, 1997; Hood, 2012; Klein et al., 2011; Loftus, 1976; Marcus, 2008; Schacter, 2002). We think memory is, by and large, an accurate record of the past (Simons & Chabris, 2011). But accuracy—as research on human recall and courtroom testimony has long shown—is not something human memory is very good at (Loftus & Ketcham, 1991).

As we are having an experience, we make decisions (some conscious, some not) about which aspects of the experience are relevant or important to pay attention to, which are less so, and which can be ignored as unimportant or irrelevant. When we store the memory in long-term memory (LTM), we store, not a full record of the experience, but a record of what we have paid attention to. We can even add elements to the memory that we did not actually experience by making inferences based on our previous experiences.

LTM is a repository of edited versions of our past experiences. We use these memories, among other things, for three important functions: One is to *make sense* of the things and events around us. Another is to *prepare for future action* by recalling what has happened in the past. Both these tasks work better if we have had a lot of relevant experience of sufficient variety to lead to accurate expectations and inferences. Too little or too narrow experience is good neither for sense-making or preparing for future choices and actions. The third function of our memories is to tell others and ourselves "our story," the story of who we are, what we have done, and how we look at the world (Gazzaniga, 2011; Hood, 2012). This story—which changes with time—is a large part of what gives us a sense of unity, uniqueness, and coherence, despite all the changes we have been through in life.

As an example of how we use memories to make sense of new encounters, let me use something that happened to me recently. Not long ago I moved to a rural area to engage in farming. A few days ago, when I entered a restaurant, I saw a large group of people eating together with birthday balloons around their tables. The people were from three different generations. To make sense of this situation, I formed expectations based on my past experience.

The people in the restaurant reminded me of the hard-working, family-centered, sober, lower-middle-class extended families I knew growing up. I thought, here is an extended family celebrating someone's birthday. These are the not-rich-not-poor, struggling, but surviving, Americans of my youth, a group now threatened with extinction, as upward mobility has all but disappeared in the United States.

It turned out that my prediction was both wrong and right and in an illuminating way. They were not an extended family. They were all members of Alcoholics Anonymous, celebrating the "birthdays" of some of the group members' sobriety.

But, in a sense, they *were* an extended family. And hard work was indeed what it took to beat their addiction (I was thinking this at the restaurant while drinking a glass of wine). And, of course, they were sober.

Throughout this book, I will point out that today people often organize into spaces where they bond over a shared affinity (for these people, AA), and not big categories such as race, class, gender, or ability (Gee, 2013). The people in the restaurant were of different ages, but they were "peers" in just the way all the different sorts of people devoted to anime fan fiction, say, are peers, regardless of age or other classificatory differences. Despite my academic "knowledge"—and even despite having once read about AA as a sort of affinity space (Holland et al., 1998)—I brought my memories of families rather than my academic knowledge to bear.

So my memories worked and didn't work. And the new experience is now a new memory that will interact with my old ones to change my future expectations and sense-making activities. This is how we humans make sense, from the past forward via experience but, hopefully, on the lookout to learn something new when our initial expectations turn out to be wrong.

We use memories to form expectations not only to make sense of what is going on around us but also so that we can be prepared to act in new situations. For example, I have been a professor at seven different universities. Each time I move I have to use my memories of dealing with deans and academic institutions to prepare for how to act and interact in the new situation. How should I respond to an offer? What should I ask for? How should I work with new administrators? How much should I trust them? If my expectations turn out to be correct, then I will have been well prepared and, perhaps, saved myself some grief.

If my expectations, however, turn out to be wrong, I, as would all humans, will face a crucial decision: Should I let this new situation change how I form expectations based on my past dealings with deans and institutions? If I do, perhaps I have learned something. Or should I treat the new situation as an aberration and remain firm in my expectations for the future? Or, worse yet, should I just act on my wrong expectations and simply ignore the evidence that I am wrong?

What I have called *committed testers* will default to the first case and use their failed expectations to reflect on the expectations and perspectives they bring to bear on new experiences. Failed expectations, and reflection on why they failed, are key to learning (Harford, 2011; Popper, 1994). But we need to be aware of the expectations we bring and the past experiences on which they are based, and we must be ready, too, to acknowledge when they have failed, and reflect and learn.

Finally, we story our lives to ourselves and others by using our memories to tell our own narratives. We are usually the "hero" of our stories of self. Our stories change with time, but the fact that we are the agent and protagonist of our own story gives us a sense of a unified self. Though, in reality, people take on different identities across time and space and act and think differently in different contexts, failing to feel ourselves as somehow unified and coherent can lead to mental illness (Gee, 2013; Hood, 2012). It is a "necessary fiction."

As we use memories for sense-making, preparing for future action, and storying ourselves, and as we add new memories to old ones, our memories get revised. This is what leads to our memories being better for meaning-making, preparation for future action, and storying than for factual accuracy. We are often better at noticing this in others than in ourselves. I have an identical twin brother, and I have watched him report memories and tell stories over the years about our shared past that have changed sometimes in small ways and sometimes in large ones. I am sure he would say the same thing of me. And, indeed, our memories have diverged more and more over the years as we have used them in our different contexts in life.

A NOTE ON THE BRAIN

Psychologists talk about the brain as if it were a computer, an information-processing device. We saw in the preceding chapter that this is misleading. The human brain is embodied; that is, it is inside a body and part of that body. It thinks and feels by using experience as its "fuel" (Bergen, 2012; Clark, 1997; Damasio, 1999; Gallese, 2007; Gallistel & King, 2010; Tomasello, 2014; M. Wilson, 2002).

We academics use statements like "The brain stores memories" and The brain stores information." We say that "the brain manipulates symbols or representations." All this is, indeed, what computers do. But it is probably not what brains do.

In this book, this sort of language is just a metaphor. When I say that a memory is "stored," I just mean it is available somehow for use. I have no idea—and nor does anyone else—where it is in the brain. The memory is almost certainly not in one "place" and is likely the product of an interaction of many different parts or actions of the brain.

The reality is that we do not yet know how the brain engages with memory and information. It is certainly not a container or hard drive that stores things, each in its own place. However the brain does manage to retain and revise memories of past experience, though, we do know that memory is interactive: Old memories interact and adapt to one another and to new memories. It is a growing, living system.

While we do not know what is "in" the brain (or even what "in" would really mean here), we do, nonetheless, know some things about the effects of the brain, body, and world working interactively together. We well know, for example, that high levels of stress (a chemical, social, and physical thing) are very bad for our brains, our bodies, and our interactions with the world and with other people (Hannaford, 2005; Pickett & Wilkinson, 2011).

EDITING EXPERIENCES

It was noted above that we edit an experience when we store it in memory in terms of what we took to be relevant and important. This is what we paid attention to. Much else was backgrounded or left out of the memory. What determines what we find relevant and important? This is largely a social affair. We learn from different social contexts (families, cultures, interest groups, institutions, and so forth) what is worth paying the most attention to—what to focus on—in different sorts of experiences in life. Of course, our own unique personalities, desires, and values affect how we edit an experience, as well. Two people can have the same experience, even together but store quiet different versions of it in long-term memory.

A striking example of how radically humans can edit an experience is seen in an experiment where people watched a video and missed a woman in a gorilla suit (Chabris & Simons, 2009). People were asked to watch a short video where six people, three in white shirts and three in black shirts, passed basketballs around. They were told to keep a silent count of the number of passes made by the people in white shirts. At one point, a woman in a gorilla suit walks into the middle of the action, faces the camera, pounds her chest, and then leaves. The gorilla spends nine seconds on screen. Remarkably, half the people who watched the video missed the gorilla. For them, the gorilla was invisible. When they were told later that they had missed the gorilla, they were incredulous.

The gorilla experiment shows dramatically that where we direct our attention determines what we see and remember. It is quite possible that the people who failed to notice the gorilla did see it in some unconscious sense, but they did not process it and retain it in the edited version of their memory. This experiment makes us wonder what else our cultures, social groups, interests, and desires make us see and make us miss.

Let us call all the edited and ever-being-revised experiences in our long-term memory our "experience resource base." As I have pointed out, we use this resource base for sense-making, preparing for new encounters, and storying the self. All of these are capacities of the mind/brain with their own strengths and weaknesses (in all of us).

SENSE-MAKING/PATTERN RECOGNITION

Humans are attracted to meaningfulness (Gazzaniga, 1988, 2011; Gee, 2013; Hood, 2012). Most people badly need to know *why* things have happened, and do not like to think that things, especially very good or very bad things, are just random events, with no real meaning beyond that of chance. We want to know that things happen for a reason. We want to know what things mean and what they might portend for the future.

We want, and even need, to know these things so that we can make sense of our lives and prepare for the future. When we feel that the things we experience have no discernible meaning, we humans often get sick in mind and body. We feel a loss of control over our lives and destinies.

For example, consider a woman who was getting married and had to move up the date of her wedding by five months because her husband was called up for military service (for data, see Schiffrin, 1987, pp. 49–50; see also Gee, 2014). Her father attended the wedding, but died a week later. About these events, the woman remarked in an interview, "And I just felt that move [moving the wedding up] was meant to be, because if not, he [her father] wouldn't have been there. So y'know it just seems that that's how things work out."

Like most of us, this woman wants to feel that things "happen for a reason." She sees a purposeful connection between the event of her husband being called up for service and the fact that her father got to see her married before he died. It is as if some beneficent force "made" it all happen for the "good."

We make sense by connecting things, making inferences, and finding patterns in our edited experiences. If we read, "The king died, then the queen died," we want to find a connection between the events. We are quite likely to infer that the queen died because the king died, the queen dying perhaps from grief (Forster, 1927).

Pattern recognition is an important part of the human sense-making capacity. Humans are pattern recognizers par excellence (Ackerman, 2005; Gee, 2013; Margolis, 1987). Pattern recognition is, in fact, our superpower as beings. We seek for and find patterns and subpatterns everywhere in our experiences, even when the patterns don't really exist—for example, some people find patterns in the stars and connect them back meaningfully to human events.

Our human sense-making capacity is essential to our survival. However, we often care more about whether the meanings we attribute to things and events give us emotional comfort than we do about whether they are true or not (Buonomano, 2011; Gazzaniga, 1988, 2011; Gee, 2013; Hood, 2012). Yet, especially in the modern world, with all its complexity, dangers, and risks, it can be dangerous to ignore reality.

The human sense-making capacity often needs to be reined in. Sometimes it needs to be subordinated more than usual to evidence and to discussions with others who have different interpretations of things. Indeed, this should be a core function of education.

One of many "bugs" that psychologists have found in human sense-making is called *confirmation bias* (Buonomano, 2011; Kahneman, 2011; Macknit & Martinez-Conde, 2010). What this means is that all of us are quite prone to looking for and considering only evidence that supports what we already believe. We tend to pay less attention (or none at all) to, and even dismiss, any evidence that does not fit with our beliefs. We sometimes take information that actually does not support our beliefs and misinterpret it to match up with our pre-existing expectations. Highly educated people, it turns out, are just as prone to confirmation bias, if not more so, than less educated people (Kida, 2006). This means that education is not educating, in the sense of producing what I have called committed testers.

Most humans will always have and need "comfort stories," that is, interpretations of things and events that are more for mental comfort than they are for evidential arguments (Gee, 2013). But in a pluralistic world where some people's comfort causes discomfort for others (e.g., the idea that some groups of people are inherently inferior to others), we need to teach people how to deal with uncertainty, with some-times being wrong, and with the need to test their beliefs against the world's responses (evidence) and other people's arguments.

COMMITTED TESTERS

Properly reined in, pattern recognition is crucially important for learn-ing in and out of school. Human beings tend to learn bottom-up, mov-ing from the concrete to the more general (Barsalou, 2009; diSessa, 2000; Gee, 2004; Margolis, 1987). We begin, when young or when new to a domain, with limited concrete experiences in the world and, of necessity, use these to make sense of things. However, as we get more and more experiences in the world, we seek and find patterns and subpatterns across the different elements of these experiences.

When they are accurate, these patterns and subpatterns constitute more general and abstract knowledge. They constitute general rules, principles, and procedures that we rely on and follow. When the pro-cedure for seeking, finding, and testing patterns is formalized, we call it science. Since pattern recognition is key to the general beliefs and principles we will live by, it is crucial that people, young and old, learn to test the patterns they find in and the principles they infer from new experiences, in critical discussion with other people who may see things differently.

This point is crucial, and I will return to it later in this book. We live in a world that faces many crises, is changing fast, and is risky and riven with ideological and religious conflicts. In such a world, people need to be committed testers.

Committed testers are aware that humans are frail and that ignorance is a continent and knowledge is but a small village. They are committed, as a moral form of life, to testing their perspectives (interpretations, reasoning, sense-making, and pattern recognition) against evidence and in critical discussions with others in a common journey toward truth and peace (at least as close as we humans can get to them).

Committed testers seek to be aware of confirmation bias, and they fight against it by actively seeking evidence that does not support their beliefs and actively trying to falsify their beliefs. They will commit to beliefs that only have stood the rigors of such tests and even then only tentatively, as they stay open to new evidence and new perspectives (Popper, 1994).

All humans, of course, sometimes test their perspectives, especially when these are manifestly not working. But few human beings are committed testers—willing to leave their comfort zones—unless they have been well taught and mentored. At heart, this is what a modern education should be about.

People need to be lifelong deliberate learners, self-teachers, and committed testers. The reason for this is that the world today is too dangerous and risky—and there are too many people and institutions in it that do not always wish others well—for us to be naive enough to think that any of us can safely and morally live an unexamined life.

MEMORY AS FUTURE-ORIENTED: IMAGINATION

As we have seen, memory is often future-oriented in the sense that we use our memories of past experience to form expectations and prepare for action in new encounters (Klein et al., 2010, 2011). The capacity that allows us to do this is imagination. Imagination draws on our record of edited experiences to prepare us for future actions and choices. We call up old experiences, and reflect on what has happened in the past, before we act and face the consequences in the real world.

We recall what has happened in the past, and the sense we have made of it, and then ask ourselves what this all implies about what we should or should not expect and do now in a new experience. Of course, we can compare and contrast multiple and different memories of past experience (if we have had enough diverse experiences) to reflect on various possibilities about what we should expect and how we should act.

Human memory is, in a sense, more *future-oriented* than it is past-oriented. We often edit our past experiences based on how we hope to make good use of these experiences in the future to accomplish our goals and desires. And as we act in the world, if certain memories work well for preparation for future action, we tend to care more about how well they have worked for our survival and success and somewhat less about how "accurate" they are as a veridical record of the past.

Human imagination is a simulation device. It allows us to use memories to play out various scenarios in the theater of our minds before we act. It even allows us to role-play as others to reflect on their motives and possible reactions. When we use our edited memories of past experience for future planning and action, we do not have to rely only on information about what (we think) actually happened in the past. Since imagination is a powerful simulation device, it can cut and paste aspects from different experiences we have had—including media we have consumed—to make up situations that have never happened and maybe never could.

We can easily imagine a pig and bird (if we have experience of both) and make up a flying pig. And, of course, some smart people, that is, inventors, in the past actually made metal tubes that could fly (planes), because they could imagine them well before they had ever actually experienced them.

Our use of memories to make sense of things and to prepare for the future can be more or less elaborate. These processes often happen at a fairly low level of conscious awareness as elements of memories are triggered by what we see and feel in a new situation. But the process can be—and often should be—more overt, elaborate, and conscious. Otherwise, we too often let the past be too rigid a guide to the future.

So a child has experiences, edits them, stores them, and then uses them as preparation for future action (uses them to simulate possibilities and plans in his or her mind). These uses change the memory, and thus the child's record of the past becomes, as for all of us, storied and rich with patterns, inferences, and revisions, not simply "neutral" and "true." Furthermore, a child's success in life—and growth as a human—depends more on imagination (memory as future-focused) than on memory as an accurate historical record.

All this is not meant to imply that what actually happened in the past is unimportant. That is why we have historians and don't just leave knowledge of the past to our individual and ever-changing memories of past experiences. Truth is important, but smart humans know that truth is a journey that requires tools, collaboration with others, and research, not only simple trust in our own memories.

Schools are often too focused on getting students to memorize what they have read and heard, or at least to be able to recall these things on a test. Educators are often too little focused (if at all) on memory as a database for preparation for action and a better future.

Our imaginations allow us to conjure up and reflect on actions we cannot actually take or at least take here and now. Imagination is thus a source not just of planning and forethought but also of hopes, dreams, and active preparation for making new futures for ourselves, if need be. In and out of school, we badly need to think about how experience, talk, texts, and media can fuel the imagination as a guide to future action, hopes, and possibilities.

The fact that imagination uses long-term memory as its fuel source is crucially important. If people, young or old, have stored memories of their past experiences in edited forms that are dysfunctional, this can be a long-term and serious problem. For example, children under a great deal of stress because of poverty, abuse, or chaos are overly vigilant in the attention they pay to any possible source of harm or risk in their experiences (Hannaford, 2005; Pollak, Vardi, Putzer Bechner, & Curtin, 2005; Tough, 2012). They pay vivid attention to these elements of their experiences, even if they are not very real possibilities, at the expense of other important aspects of those experiences. As edited memories—overfocused as they are on possible sources of harm— such experiences do not serve them well for imagining new positive possibilities, for seeking new powers, or for persisting past failure to replan and act again.

Such endangered children need both new experiences and new ways to edit their former and future experiences. This requires lowering their stress levels and therefore speaking to poverty, abuse, and chaos and not just to "school reform."

All of us can do and have done a good deal of dysfunctional editing. We have often habituated what we pay attention to and what we don't, rather than being open to new possibilities. Committed testers seek out opportunities to re-edit (rethink) their memories and new ways to edit new ones. But, of course, we all need help (teachers, mentors, good resources, and new experiences) here. It is often hard to undo aspects of powerful memories.

CHOICE

We use the edited records of experience in long-term memory as a database (which we revise and update over time) both to think about and make sense of the past and to think about and act in the future. People who have had a diverse and deep array of experiences in the world, and who have edited them well, tend to make good choices. And they can re-think and re-plan well when they don't. Isn't this really what we want for our children and ourselves: the ability to make good choices and recover well from bad ones?

The psychologist Dan Schwartz has argued that when we think about school and assessment we too often focus on knowledge (Schwartz & Arena, 2013). But choice, he claims, is a more important notion. People who can make good choices in a given domain (e.g., romance, science, gaming, gardening) have lots of well-organized knowledge about that domain. So being able to make good choices implies and correlates with having deep knowledge.

However, people can have lots of knowledge, in the sense of knowing lots of facts, but not be able to put this knowledge to good use to make good choices. Their knowledge is not well organized in the service of making good choices and engaging in fruitful problem solving, though it may be well organized for passing paper-and-pencil tests of retention and recall.

To have a powerful and effective imagination, people must have had diverse and deep experiences and must have stored, edited, and integrated them in their minds in effective ways for making sense of them and for preparing for future action. A powerful and effective imagination, in turn, means that people have organized their record of experience (their experience base in LTM) well enough to make good choices and recover from bad ones in new experiences.

When Dan Schwartz first suggested that choice was a more important skill to teach and assess than knowledge (because, in fact, being able to make good choices correlates with and implies knowledge, but knowledge does not always correlate with or imply being able to make good choices) he scandalized many educators (and certainly displeased test-makers). But his claim, like many really smart ideas, seems obvious once you have heard it and have really thought about it outside the strictures of our normal intellectual silos.

Furthermore, imagination and choice are clearly closely related. We cannot make good choices in novel situations unless we can imagine different choices and reflect on what results they each might lead to. We cannot try again when we fail if we cannot imagine good alternatives. Developing memory in its role of focusing on the past and not also on its role as fodder for future planning and action can leave a child with a head full of "knowledge" but no ability to make good choices and imagine new possibilities.

Children and adults do not learn to be good choosers all by themselves. They need teachers and mentors who design good experiences for them and guide them through these experiences by helping them to know what to pay attention to. They need teachers and mentors to model for them how to use the past to make the future better by reflecting, planning, and simulating, both in their minds and in discussions with others, before they act in the world. Good sense-making, good imaginations, and good choices don't just happen or grow "naturally." They are made socially and are part and parcel of a good education.

Let me close this chapter with a hard question about the future that we will have to return to later. How do young people, based on their past experiences, prepare for the future if the future itself (thanks to rapid change) is more unpredictable now than it has ever been before (Taleb, 2006, 2012)? What if past experience works less and less well today as a guide to the future than it ever has in history?

It has always been true that people who know and understand possible future trajectories through society's groups and institutions are heavily advantaged in making better futures for themselves. Their social and institutional knowledge is a map that helps them orient as they move into the future.

For example, when I did research in a struggling postindustrial city, many of the schoolchildren (White, Brown, and Black) who were interviewed for the study were poor. They would say things like "I want to be a vet because I want to groom animals." When asked if there was a difference between Harvard University (which was in their state) and their local state college they said, "No, a college is a college." When asked what they needed to get out of school to go to college, they responded that they did not know. Many of their teachers recommended the technical high school over the regular high school, despite the fact, as we later discovered, that most of the local employers would not hire people from the tech high school because its technology was so out of date.

Much more privileged children, from a wealthy town in the same state, in our interviews could name the institutions and professions that constituted the landmarks on their trajectory toward success in society. They knew exactly what was needed at each level of schooling to get to the next and what school had to do with professions and powerful institutions in society. They saw society as a clear map of possibilities that they could attain. On the downside, these wealthy students had a deep fear that they might fall off the escalator to success, crowded as it is, and thus fail to become a "worthwhile" human being on their families' terms.

Today, however, work, wages, job security, and institutions are changing radically and will do so yet more in the future (Ford, 2015). We will discuss these issues further later in this book. In the United States today there is more downward than upward mobility. There is a greater degree of inequality than ever before. And well-educated people fear losing their good jobs when they get to be 45 or so and younger workers are cheaper and more up to date (Stiglitz, 2013). At the same time, more and more people are finding meaning, and sometimes making money, "off market" and outside any formal institution (Shirky, 2008, 2010). The future is a more foreign continent than it has ever been before. The map keeps changing.

CHAPTER 4

Play and Talk

PLAYFUL EXPERIENCE

In Chapter 2 we argued that children, and adults new to a domain, learn first and best from +experiences. These are experiences where a person has an action to take and cares about the outcome and where attention is well-managed. There is, however, a particularly important type of experience we have not yet talked about. This type of experience is *play*.

Playful experiences, like +experiences, often involve acting, caring, and focusing attention, but in the context of imaginative play. Young children's play often involves pretending to engage in meaningful actions where focused attention is required. Children play house, take care of doll babies, pretend to be teachers, act out social encounters with imaginary friends, and save the world as superheroes. Play shows us that caring and an affective attachment to what you are doing does not have to be serious.

There is a video game I love that came out several years ago. It is called *Chibi-Robo*. In the game you play as a four-inch house-cleaning robot. You have to clean the whole house, top to bottom, but are only four inches tall. As a player you come to look at house-cleaning in a whole new way, as you work out strategies to get everywhere and do your job.

Such games, often made in Japan (as *Chibi-Robo* is), involve doing everyday tasks in an imaginative universe. It is odd they are so much fun, for children and even for some adults like me. They let children play at "real" things and they let older children and adults see mundane things in new ways. Making the mundane "strange" again—the way we saw it before it became routine—is one of the key functions of art.

Play, of course, changes the character of acting, caring, and attention in comparison to more serious experiences. Nonetheless, playful experiences and more serious ones share the feature that, at their best, they can put people into a state of "flow" (Csikszentmihályi, 1990). In a state of flow people forget about time and lose themselves in an experience. When this happens, the distinction between playful and serious becomes quite blurred. It is why some people look at their work as play.

Why is play so powerful for early learning? Because play frees us from the fear of failure, allows us to take risks, to explore, and to try new things. Play allows us to see not just the way things are but also how they could be (Brown & Vaughn, 2009; Elkind, 2007).

Play, and even just imagination (as in daydreaming), allows us not just to be who we are at one point in time but also to try on new identities and new roles and grow into new ways of being human. Because of these features, play is important for adults and not just children, especially if the former want to become what we earlier called committed testers. One good way to test your assumptions and beliefs is to give them up in a playful environment where you are free to take risks, try new things, and see how things look then.

VERTICAL AND HORIZONTAL LEARNING: THE IMPORTANCE OF MUCKING AROUND

Schools—and too many current early childhood practices meant to "accelerate" children—stress vertical learning at the expense of horizontal learning. Vertical learning involves moving ever up a skill tree from lower to higher skills. Vertical learning is, of course, important, but too often we move learners up the skill tree too fast. Good learning requires good horizontal learning as well.

Horizontal learning (Goto, 2003) involves engaging in activities and skills without worrying about ratcheting up a skill tree. Time pressure is lowered. In horizontal learning the learner explores the lay of the land and tries out various possibilities, takes risks, and "mucks around." This process deepens the learner's perspectives on skills and their contexts of application. It prepares them to ratchet up the skill tree when they are ready and well-prepared to do so, with a sense that they can do it and know what it all means.

Mucking around, at its best, is a form of play and serves much the same function. It allows children to take risks, try different things, and fail without a high cost. In school, we too often ignore the fact that some children have had a lot of horizontal learning at home and we move everyone in the class quickly up the skill tree, forgetting that some children may not have had enough horizontal learning yet. We are not willing to allow these children the time they need for "mucking around," but that does not lessen its necessity or importance.

By the way, in the case of literacy learning, horizontal learning is often called *emergent literacy* (Rhyner, 2009). In emergent literacy, children muck around playfully with sounds and rhymes, with letters and words, with being read to and engaging in pretend readings of their own, and with all sorts of connections between books and the world forged via media and in talk and interaction with adults. The literacy research is clear: Good literacy learning requires hours of rich emergent literacy practices starting at home (Adams, 1990; Dickinson, 1994; Dickinson & Neuman, 2003, 2006). These hours cannot simply be skipped in the service of moving forward quickly to meet policymakers' curriculum goals and guidelines.

Even scientists and other professionals muck around. When experts take on a new challenge, beyond skills that have become routine, they become novices again and must engage in horizontal learning in the new area. Unfortunately, too many supposed experts rest on their laurels and do not continually seek out new challenges that will allow them, after a course of new learning, to ratchet up their skills to even higher levels (Bereiter & Scardamalia, 1993). The process requires being willing to play around and risk (even invite) failure again. Good learners in any area, no matter how expert they are, take time to play around with things to see if they can get new ideas and insights or break intellectual logjams.

TALK

In the preceding chapter I stressed the power of imagination to prepare us for action. We can use our memories of past experience to simulate possibilities in our mind before we act in the world and face the consequences. This capacity is much more limited in animals than it is in humans. The reason it is so expansive in humans is language.

Animals can anticipate things, but they cannot predict such possibilities as "what might happen tomorrow at an important meeting if I get drunk tonight and don't get a good 8 hours of sleep." To imagine such things requires not just past experiences but also language (and culture).

Language allows us humans to sort, classify, and compare and contrast past experiences and patterns and subpatterns we have found in those experiences. It allows us, through talk and texts, to share in other people's experiences and, thus, vastly expand our experiential resource base. And it allows us to learn how to think about and reflect on our experiences and the uses we make of them to prepare for the future.

Talk of a certain sort between children and adults is a crucial source of early learning and development (Dickinson, 1994; Dickinson & Neuman, 2006; Gardner-Neblett & Gallagher, 2013; Hart & Risely, 1995; Snow, 1991). The sort of talk I am referring to I will call *nurturing experiential talk*. Children learn from playful and serious experiences in the world. But they learn how to think about and reflect on these experiences from nurturing talk and interaction with adults.

What I am calling nurturing experiential talk is interactive talk about experience—the adult's, someone else's, or the child's. It is not talk that is primarily instructions, reprimands, or commands. It is nurturing only if it is carried out in contexts where there is an emotional bond and trust between the adult and the child.

Nurturing talk is made up of stories about experience, commentaries on how one thought and felt in an experience, tales of success and failure, and ideas about what it is important to pay attention to in certain sorts of experiences. It is dialogue with children about what they thought about or how they felt or acted in an experience; what worked out, what didn't, and why; and what other things could have been done. It is commentary on experiences others have had or ones that have been depicted in books and other media. With young children, it is also dialogic interactive talk around books and other media and their connections to the world.

Such talk is best for learning and development when it is *topically sustained* (Snow, 1986). By this I mean talk that stays on one topic for a while and develops that topic through dialogue with the child. Such talk requires both parties, child and adult, to use complex language and thinking to connect and integrate information germane to one topic across several or many turns at talk (Snow, 1986). Sometimes too much of the talk children hear from adults is either instructions and reprimands or some form of 20 questions, where no one topic is developed and expanded over time.

Negotiation is one good form of topically sustained dialogic talk with children, as long as it does not occur in an "anything goes," too permissive environment. Negotiation often also requires appeals to experience, expectations, and outcomes. Of course, storytelling and other forms of sharing and comparing experiences are excellent as well.

Nurturing experiential conversation between adults and children is foundational to the development of children's skills for editing experiences well for long-term memory and for building up their imaginative capacities. In turn, we have seen that a child's imaginative capacity is crucial for future planning, making good choices, and imagining new possibilities.

IMAGINATION

Imagination is important because it is our imaginations that are the foundation for all our abilities to plan, hypothesize, prepare, assess, and hope. The core of human intelligence is to imagine and plan things in our minds before we act in the world. But we can do this only if our imaginative capacities are well-developed.

As we become adults, our capacity to prepare intelligently for action, to adapt to change, and to engage in smart strategies is key to our success and survival in life. And this capacity is our imagination, the theater in our minds. Its foundations are +experiences; playful experiences; nurturing, topically sustained talk with adults about experience; and horizontal learning (mucking around).

One reason adult talk is so important for children is that such talk can teach children how to think about and reflect on their playful and more serious experiences in the world and in media. They thereby gain metaknowledge, that is, the ability to think and talk about experiences—their own and others'—and not just have experiences. They learn, as well, from adult talk and examples, how to make their imaginative preparations for action and problem solving all the more effective.

Talk with parents (or other primary caregivers) about experience is particularly important for young children. Such talk takes place as part and parcel of children's early socialization in life as a member of a family and community. As a result, what is said and meant is heavily charged with positive affect (feeling, emotion) for the child, unless the child has lost trust in the parents. Such heavily charged information is stored more deeply in long-term memory, and remains more central, even if unconsciously so, for a long time, often a lifetime. When the learning that children do in their primary socialization in life is not emotionally charged with love and trust, the child's development and sense of belonging and mattering can be deeply harmed (Davidov & Grusec, 2006; Gray et al., 2002).

How parents help children to think about (process, edit) experiences in the world and in media, and how they teach children what it is important to pay attention to (what matters and why), are the foundation of the child's initial and enduring perspectives on (theories about) the world. All later learning is layered onto this foundation, and this foundation deeply affects that later learning. If the foundation is not solid or not finished, the child needs help. That help will involve teachers and mentors designing good +experiences and meaningful play opportunities for the child, allowing time for horizontal learning at each level of learning, and lots of nurturing experiential dialogic talk with adults or more advanced peers.

TALK, TEXTS, AND MEDIA

Children learn (initially) from both playful and serious experiences in the world. But young people can have only so many and certain types of experiences in the world, both because of safety concerns and because of opportunity. There are things they can't or shouldn't do in the real world.

Stories, texts, and media (e.g., videos, films, music, and video games) can be important means for extending children's real-world experiences. Each of these can cause a child to fill up his or her imagination with images and match them to words, just as children do in real-world experiences. Talk, texts, and media are types of virtual or *vicarious experiences.*

The human mind is built in such a way that people (that is, all of us) often cannot remember whether an experience of theirs was in the world, in talk (in a story for example), in a text, or in a movie (Reeves & Nass, 1999). All these can become fodder for pattern recognition, the superpower of the human mind.

However, humans are also made (have evolved) in such a way that experiences in the world (especially +experiences) and face-to-face talk are the most primordial, foundational, and important sources for learning, development, and nurturing (Levinas, 1969). Embodied experiences in the real world and face-to-face talk are never going to be replaced for humans, and a lack of either or both is not good for physical or emotional health and well-being, especially for children.

Good talk, texts, and media expose children to a wider array of experiences. In turn, children use these new, but vicarious, experiences to broaden the real-world experiences they actively seek out. As they broaden and deepen their real-world experiences, they can gain more from new and more advanced talk, texts, and media and then bring these lessons back home again to their real-world experiences. It is a virtuous cycle. But it does not happen all by itself.

When parents, mentors, and teachers create *transactions* and *connections* between real-world experiences and talk, texts, and various forms of media, they are engaged in one of the most crucial aspects of child development (Gee, 2004; New London Group, 1996; Rosenblatt, 2005). Such transactions and connections integrate children's real-world experiences and vicarious experiences into a well-organized and highly integrated experiential resource base for thinking about the past, making sense of things, preparing for the future, and storying the self in healthy ways. In such a well-connected and well-integrated resource base, literacy, media, and the world are deeply connected and enrich one another.

If you do an Internet search of "texts to world connections" or "texts to self connections," what you get, predictably, are lots of school worksheet activities where students fill in blanks with short phrases connecting parts of a text to the world or their own lives. This is *not* what I am talking about when I stress the importance of connections among the texts, the world, and the lived reality of the reader.

I am talking about young people standing in the world outside school being helped to relate what they are experiencing to texts they have read and vice versa. I am talking about students reading texts in school and explicating them in extended talk about themselves; experiences they have had; and what they know from talk, texts, and media of the world we all share. I am talking about adults and peers engaging in extended dialogue about how the world, experiences in life, and different people's different lived realities relate to texts and vice versa. The earlier this starts, the better.

For some children literacy is not as affectively (emotionally) and cognitively tied to the world of experience (and vice versa) as it is for others. For these children, literacy is isolated. It is a domain with which the child does not truly affiliate and where the child's connections to empowerment as an actor in the world are unfelt and unseen.

These unfortunate results occur when transactions and connections among the world, talk, texts, and media are not made early and sustained later.

Such children often have problems with literacy at school. The remedy is the same: lots of good playful and serious +experiences; lots of good vicarious experiences via talk, texts, and media; lots of nurturing experiential talk with an adult in an emotionally positive relationship; and help in making transactions across and connections among real-world experiences, talk, texts, and media of all sorts.

Remember here, too, the importance of horizontal learning (mucking around). There is no need to stress being a "good reader" too early and too much, to the detriment of the sorts of emotional attachments, experiences, talk, and media that are the foundation of reading's meaningfulness and significance to the child.

Now, many of my readers, especially if they are teachers working under today's testing pressures, will say, "We cannot take the time to do all that. These children are too far behind. They have to move up the skill tree and fast, so they can pass the test. There is no time to let them 'play around' and risk failure."

But alas, that is not how humans are built or how human learning and development actually work. You can't make your pet cat fly just because some policymaker demands you do so. That is not how cats are made. You can, indeed, get kids to pass tests, but that does not ensure that they have the wherewithal to flourish in life and society. Our only moral alternative is to do the best we can and to seek continually to engage everyone in conversations about the reality of children and development before a great many more children are damaged.

Children who have not formed an affective affiliation to literacy and its connections to the world early on are often not just behind in reading; they can also be filled with fears and doubts about and even hostility toward literacy. Their "affective filter"—the mechanism that allows humans to block inputs that they feel might harm or shame them—goes up when we ask them to read, and especially when we ask them to write (Dickinson & Neuman, 2003, 2006; Krashen, 1982).

When this happens no remedy is going to work unless and until we reduce the child's affective filter. In most cases the remedy is not "special education" of the skill-and-drill type that removes skills from their contexts of application and meaning in the world. The remedy requires building trust between the child and adults at school; a curriculum that is designed so that the child has early successes with reading and writing; close ties to the child's family and community; time for horizontal learning; a good deal of experiential talk with adults one-on-one; and all sorts of transactions and connections among talk, texts, media, and the world (Gee, 2004, 2015a).

LITERACY

Books and texts of all other sorts are parts of literacy. But what is "literacy"? Literacy, in the traditional sense, is the set of skills it takes to read and write written language. Written language is a recoding of oral language; it is a way to use a small set of symbols (letters) to encode anything that can be said into written form. Written language allows us to take oral language on the road, so to speak, and let it travel far and wide, well beyond the ephemeral reach of speech.

The development of reading and writing is closely tied, in many important ways, to oral language, something to which too many educators do not pay enough attention. The best predictor of a child's early success with reading in school is the child's *oral* vocabulary at 5 years of age (*American Educator*, 2003; Dickinson & Neuman, 2003, 2006). This does not mean that every child has a poor vocabulary in terms of everyday words. What it means is that some children get early preparation for school by hearing lots of adult talk that is full of words children will later hear in talk and see in texts at school.

Humans use the same mental capacities to comprehend oral language, written language, and the world of events (Stanovich, 2000). So for children, in particular, the upper limit of their ability to comprehend written language is set by their ability to comprehend oral language (Biemiller, 2003).

We need to keep in mind, too, that as children move to school, academic styles of language in speech and writing become more and more important. Academic styles of language are no one's native language. Compare these two sentences (Gee, 2004): "Hornworms sure vary a lot in how well they grow" and "Hornworm growth exhibits a significant amount of variation." The first sentence is in a vernacular variety of language ("everyday language"). The second is in an academic variety of language. As school goes on, academic varieties of language become more and more central to schooling and to students' affiliation with school (Gee, 2004, 2015a). Children need to hear and speak, not just read and write, such language. Unfortunately, in school we often underplay hearing and speaking academic language in favor of reading and writing it and as a result undermine students' deep comprehension of and affiliation with such language.

When we make oral language skills better, we make written language skills better. If we ignore the former—and we often do—we weaken and limit the latter. Adults talking to children in topically sustained dialogic talk about experience and the world is the best initial way to make oral language skills better. So is asking children to tell their own stories; report on their ideas and actions; and explain their desires, opinions, and choices. Thereafter, children in school need topically sustained dialogic talk in academic language. And they need to talk, listen to, read, and write such language.

The amount of one-on-one talk a child hears from an adult—especially when it is about not just the here and now but the wealth, breadth, and depth of the adult's experiences of the world—is also a very strong predictor of a child's success in school and society (Dickinson & Neuman, 2003, 2006; Hart & Risely, 1995; Snow, Burns, & Griffin, 1998). Such talk deepens children's experiences in the world by supplementing them with the experiences of adults brought to life through talk (often stories). Such talk, as it calls forth images into a child's mind, becomes a type of virtual experience and model for the child.

I want to end this chapter by forestalling a common misunderstanding. When I talk about the importance of adults' engaging in emotionally positive talk about experience with children, I do not mean only highly educated adults. All adults, rich or poor, educated or not, have had a great many experiences in life—ups and downs, surprises and disappointments, and experiences shared with others—and have attained hard-gained insights. When they talk about their experiences they are engaged in just the sorts of extended forms of talk and connection-making that are good for a child's cognitive and emotional development. When they talk in an extended way about things that are not "here and now," they use forms of language that are good preparation for school for the child.

All adults can ask children to expand on their ideas, report on things that have happened to them, argue for their viewpoints, and explain their preferences and choices. Adults do not need to go back to school to talk to and with their children. They just need to open their mouths and trust in their own worth, knowledge, and agency.

We also have to remember that to succeed in school—and certainly to make it to college—young people need mastery of, and affiliation with, academic varieties of language (Gee, 2004, 2015a; Schleppegrell, 2004). Many children from homes with well-educated parents hear the beginnings of such varieties of language at home when their parents use "the language of books" with them. They also learn to identify such language with their families' values and thus are ready and willing to affiliate with it when they see it more fully at school.

These children who have heard the beginnings of academic varieties of language at home have, for the most part, been exposed to, not technical terms tied to specific academic areas, but what are sometimes called Tier 2 words and their use in more explicit and sustained forms of language (Beck, McKeown, & Kucan, 2002). Tier 2 words are relatively high-frequency words used by adults across many different academic areas (or what school calls content areas). Some examples of Tier 2 words are *state, process, obvious, complex, perceive, system, evidence,* and *confirm.* Tier 1 words are the everyday words that everyone knows and uses a great deal. Tier 3 words are technical terms tied to specific areas of expertise.

Children who have not had a head start at home on Tier 2 words need adults at school who talk to them using Tier 2 words and model for them the power of these words to give access to lots of different academic areas. If these children's parents, regardless of their education level, have talked to and with children in topically sustained nurturing language about experience, the children are well prepared to learn academic styles of language. They have been exposed to talk that goes well beyond the here and now. They have become familiar with focused, sustained, elaborated, and relatively explicit talk. They just need to get the introduction to Tier 2 words, and the contexts in which they are used, at school that other children have had at home.

Teachers cannot skip the early steps some other children have taken at home. To do that would be as if some parents taught their children introductory Greek for a school system run in Greek and teachers skipped this introduction in the case of children who had not had it at home. That would be an unfair thing to do. And by the way, academic varieties of English use a great many words that are derived from Latin and are not the Germanic words that make up much of everyday English. In a sense, school eventually is more in Latin than it is in Germanic English.

Unfortunately, academic language in school is often inert. Too often it is detached from the work and problem solving for which various areas of academic research have developed their versions of academic language. This is like handing a person a tool but not teaching him or her how to use it. This is why school usually uses the term *content areas* rather than *academic areas*. Academic language, in school, just becomes a language with which to state inert facts and information ("content") and test for them on paper-and-pencil tests.

Any specialist variety of language, whether it is the language of a chemist or of a carpenter, exists as a set of tools to do things. When we detach academic language from talk, interaction, and problem solving—especially when we showcase it only in textbooks—we can hardly model its powers in the mind and in the world. It is not surprising, then, that many children, rich and poor, do not really affiliate with and feel comfortable with academic language. Indeed, many adults don't.

We will see later that there are many new varieties of specialist languages being invented in popular culture today. For example, the language on *Yu-Gi-Oh!* cards, and in the *Yu-Gi-Oh!* game rules, is every bit as technical and seemingly forbidding as most academic varieties of language (Gee, 2004, 2015a). Yet even young children readily master it and affiliate with it. But then they actually use it for something real that they want to do. It is, for them, a spiffy set of tools indeed.

CHAPTER 5

Talk and Language Development

LANGUAGE DEVELOPMENT

Despite claims to the contrary among some educators, oral language and written language are not acquired in the same way. Though oral language and written language are, of course, related, they are different things (Chomsky, 1986; Gee, 1994; Pinker, 1994).

Every human culture in history has had oral language. Oral language has been around long enough in human history to have been a product of evolution or, at least, to have been heavily affected by evolution, as well as by culture, of course. Not every culture has had written language. In fact, the great majority of cultures in history have not had it. Written language is only a few thousand years old, too short a time for evolution to have affected it. Written language is not a product of evolution but, rather, fully a product of human cultures and institutions (Havelock, 1976; Olson, 1977, 1996; Ong, 1982)

ORAL LANGUAGE

A child's first language (*native language*) is acquired by immersion in social interaction starting even before birth (babies can hear the intonation contours of people speaking to or around them). Some children can acquire more than one language as native languages, provided they acquire these early and as part of their socialization in a family.

Oral language is what we might call an "instinct" in humans (Pinker, 1994). Provided children have positive social interactions with primary caregivers (who these are differs across cultures), they will, barring quite serious disorders, acquire their native language without the need of any instruction or corrections (some parents do engage in these practices, but they do not matter). A baby whisked away from Brooklyn, New York, and taken to Beijing to be raised by

Chinese parents will speak Mandarin with no accent, certainly not a Brooklyn one. Older children and adults so whisked away might well learn Mandarin, but they will usually have an English accent and be recognizable as non-native speakers.

A child, again barring serious disorders, acquires his or her native language as well as any other child. There is no "better and worse" here in a grammatical sense. There are no cases of children, without serious disorders, who fail to acquire relative clauses, for example, because they are too complicated.

It is important to distinguish between syntax (grammar, the structure of sentences) and vocabulary (words). Children and adults can vary in how large their vocabularies are, but this has no influence on their knowledge of syntax (sentence structure). Vocabularies are large or small depending on how many different words children hear and need for what goes on in their lives. Furthermore, nearly all children develop perfectly good and relatively large vocabularies in terms of vernacular (everyday) words.

There are cases where people use one language (e.g., Spanish) as a home language to talk to friends and family and another (e.g., English) as a public language to talk to people outside friends and family. This is called *diglossia* and it is common across the world (Ferguson, 1959). In this situation, the home language usually has a smaller vocabulary than the public language.

Some people in a diglossic situation will say things like "I don't really know Spanish; I only speak it at home." They say things like this because many people confuse vocabulary and syntax. These Spanish speakers know the grammar of Spanish, though they know fewer words than some other Spanish speakers, because they use Spanish to talk about only certain topics with people with whom they share a good deal of knowledge.

Oral language develops well in all human beings, barring serious disorders. All healthy humans "take to it," and no one needs instruction in it. This is not so, of course, with all skills. Not everyone, even under similar circumstances, masters a musical instrument, a sport, or knowledge of science pretty much as well as anyone else with just immersion in interaction and practice and no instruction. Furthermore, while skills like reading vary by social class (poorer kids fare less well on average), acquisition of one's native language does not.

Not all healthy children learn to read equally easily with just immersion in practice and data. Indeed, about 20% of children have difficulty learning to read (Snow et al., 1998). It appears that, just by chance, some people's brains are better wired for acquiring reading than are some other people's, as appears to be true also of things like doing mathematics and playing chess.

Human brains, by the way, are so big and complex that a part of their wiring is determined by chance (Edelman, 1987). The neurons in the brain become wired in complex and idiosyncratic patterns, based on growth and experience, but also on chance connections that are then strengthened through use. No two people's brains, including those of identical twins, are wired the same way.

Differently wired brains are not better or worse. We all find some things easier to learn than others, different things for different people. Each of us needs more time and effort to learn some things than do some other people. None of this means that all people, barring serious illness, cannot learn to read, do mathematics, or play chess well; it simply means it takes more effort for some people than it does for others and more instruction than is the case for the development of a native oral (or signed) language.

Poverty affects reading independently of these issues about the brain. Since many disadvantaged children seem to be able to learn to read well outside school when they need to engage in some popular culture activity (Steinkuehler, Compton-Lilly, & King, 2010), it would appear that the problems poor children have in learning to read at school have more to do with weak or nonexistent affiliations with, and negative emotional attitudes toward, school-based literacy than they have to do with cognition and brains.

VERNACULAR AND SPECIALIST STYLES OF LANGUAGE

Every language in the world (e.g., Russian, Mandarin, English, Yupik) is spoken in different varieties or styles (Irvine, 2001; Labov, 1972). Just as there are different types of hats, each used for a different purpose, there are different styles of language used for different purposes.

People can speak informally or formally. They can speak in different geographical dialects. Some cultures even have different varieties of language for men or women. People can speak the language of medicine, gaming, or law.

Linguists have used different terms for these language varieties, but they are all too narrow to encompass all the different types of these varieties. The term *register* is probably the closest to being all-encompassing (Halliday, 1978), but it is still too narrow. I have elsewhere used the term *social language* for any distinctive style of speaking or writing in a given language (Gee, 2014). But, for the most part, I will simply use the term *variety* here (*style* would have done just as well).

Just as we could distinguish between different types of clothing in different ways (e.g., indoor vs. outdoor, formal vs. informal, work vs. leisure), there are different ways we could distinguish between different varieties of language. Here I want to work with the distinction between vernacular varieties of language and specialist varieties of language.

Vernacular varieties are used when we speak as an "everyday person," not as a specialist of any sort, to other people as "everyday people." Doctors can speak in a specialist medical language, but they also spend a good deal of their time, as we all do, speaking as everyday people to others.

Our vernacular variety is what we learn as our native language in our primary socialization in life as part of a family. Every human being is a master of a vernacular variety of language. Different social groups or cultures, even if they use the same language (e.g., English), can have different vernacular varieties; that is, they can speak somewhat different versions (dialects) of vernacular language.

People usually use their vernacular variety of language orally, but they can write in it as well. For example, personal letters and now some digital communication in social media are written in the vernacular. It is interesting to note, however, that some digital communication in social media today is more often written, especially by young people, in what I will call below a specialist variety of language (some of it is in "leet-speak" for example, a code used on the Internet, in which standard letters are often replaced by numerals or special characters).

Schools do not need to teach native speakers their own vernacular variety of language. They already know it just fine. However, vernacular varieties of language, because they are acquired as part of a person's early primary socialization into family and community, are profoundly tied to a person's sense of belonging, worth, and identity. One of the very best ways to disaffiliate a child from school is to denigrate that child's vernacular variety of language (because of dialect or anything else). It is a way of denigrating the child's family and community. It is a way, too, of forcing the child to choose between home and school in terms of who to admire and respect (Gee, 1990/2015b).

Specialist varieties of language are connected to groups and institutions with special sorts of interests and expertise. Many groups with special interests develop their own variety of language (in talk and writing); this helps the members of a group function effectively with one another to pursue their shared interests and goals.

Physicists, anime fans, gamers, lawyers, gang members, wine enthusiasts, theologians, and many, many others have their own special ways with words. Specialist varieties of language are not anyone's native language. They are acquired by immersion in groups who use them for their work, interests, or passion.

We can distinguish between two major groups of specialist languages: academic specialist varieties of languages (Schleppegrell, 2004) and nonacademic specialist varieties of language (Gee, 2015a). Biologists have their own ways of using language to do biology (and different types of biologists have different versions of it). This is true of any academic area. Schools, of course, use certain types of academic language in their subject areas (e.g., biology, algebra, science, social studies, and so forth). Young people who play the card game *Yu-Gi-Oh* also use a quite technical language that is incorporated into the game and its rules (Gee, 2004). But this specialist language is not an academic one. Here is a small example of *Yu-Gi-Oh* language:

> In order to Synchro Summon a Synchro Monster, you need 1 Tuner (look for "Tuner" next to its Type). The Tuner Monster and other face-up monsters you use for the Synchro Summon are called Synchro Material Monsters. The sum of their Levels is the Level of Synchro Monster you can Summon. (www.yugioh-card. com/lat-am/rulebook/YGO_RuleBook_EN-v8.pdf)

Academic varieties of language are connected to schools and universities. Nonacademic specialist languages are used primarily out of school. Many children have difficulty mastering (let alone liking) academic varieties of language. At the same time, children do not seem to have any difficulty acquiring nonacademic forms of specialist language out of school, if they are interested in the activities connected to the language. Yet many out-of-school specialist varieties of language are just as complicated as academic language. Perhaps we have something to learn from how children acquire (and learn to love) specialist forms of language out of school (Gee, 2014, 2015a).

IMPLICIT AND EXPLICIT LANGUAGE

In any variety of language, whether vernacular or specialist, there are more and less explicit substyles. When we speak we rarely can say all we mean "in so many words," that is, in a completely explicit form. It would take too long. We almost always rely, to some extent, on hearers' using the context in which we are speaking, and shared knowledge, to infer fully what we mean.

Though we nearly always rely on context and shared knowledge to fill out more fully what we mean, we can rely on context and shared knowledge more or less. In more explicit forms of language, we put more meaning into words and rely less on context and shared knowledge; in less explicit forms, we rely more on context and shared knowledge and put less of our meaning directly in words.

This is, of course, actually a continuum, from highly inexplicit to highly explicit language, through a number of styles in between. "Clean it up" leaves more to contextual inferencing than does "The coffee spilled; get a mop." And "The guy at table 10 spilled his cup of hot coffee all over the floor beneath his table; get the mop in the storeroom and clean the coffee up" relies yet less on contextual inferencing. Notice, too, the trade-off between explicitness and length: The more explicit we are, the more words we tend to use.

It is crucial to realize that *inexplicit* here does not mean "bad" and *explicit* does not mean "good." In some situations, too much explicitness is rude, because the speaker is ignoring what listeners already know and what they share with the speaker and is telling it to them anyway.

Less explicit forms of language, forms that are heavily contextualized, have been called "high-context" language. More explicit, less highly contextualized forms of language have been called "low-context" language. Here I am using the terms *high-context language* and *low-context language* where others (e.g., Hall, 1976) have used the terms *high/low-context cultures* or *high/low-context forms of communication*.

High-context language (less explicit language) is used when we want to be informal. It is often, too, a way of bonding with people and expressing solidarity with them. More explicit, low-context language is used with people with whom we do not share a lot of knowledge and background, when we want to be more formal, or when we want, in some situation, to express deference to, or respect for, someone, even if we know the person well (Labov, 1972; Milroy, 1991).

Let me give an example of how explicit and less explicit forms of language relate to formality/informality and solidarity/deference. A former student of mine once recorded herself talking to her boyfriend and to her parents about a story we had studied in class. She wanted to see how her speech differed when she spoke to each party.

In the story we had talked about in class—a story used for values-clarification tasks in psychology (readers are asked to rank the characters in the story from worst to best)—a woman named Abigail wants to get across a river to see her lover, Gregory. A riverboat captain, Roger, says he will take her only if she sleeps with him. In desperation she does so, only to see her true love, Gregory. But when she arrives and tells Gregory what happened, he disowns her and sends her away. There is more to the story (Abigail seeks revenge), but this is enough for our purposes here.

In explaining to her parents, at dinner, why she thought Gregory was the worst character in the story, the young woman said the following:

> Well, when I thought about it, I don't know, it seemed to me that Gregory should be [ranked as] the most offensive. He showed no understanding for Abigail, when she told him what she was forced to do. He was callous. He was hypocritical, in the sense that he professed to love her, then acted like that.

In her talk to her boyfriend, in an intimate setting, she had also explained why she thought Gregory was the worst character. In this context she said:

> What an ass that guy was, you know, her boyfriend. I should hope, if ever I did that to see you, you would shoot the guy. He uses her and he says he loves her.

> Roger never lies, you know what I mean?

Note how her language to her parents is more explicit and more "school-like." She is treating her parents with deference or respect on this occasion. Her language to her boyfriend is less explicit and leaves more for the boyfriend to infer from context. She is treating her boyfriend as a peer and expressing bonding or solidarity with him. Of course, in different contexts she may well have spoken differently both to her parents and to her boyfriend.

Because inexplicit forms of language are associated with solidarity and explicit forms with status and deference, both forms are connected to politeness and judgments about how to relate to others in different situations. Expressing solidarity where we should express deference or expressing deference where we should express solidarity can lead to serious problems.

Even scientists talking in a lab meeting, for example, will use less explicit, high-context forms of talk with their colleagues. They trade heavily on shared context (the lab, diagrams, and so forth) and shared background knowledge to get the job done faster and more effectively (without having to spell everything out) and to show solidarity with one another and their field (Ochs, Gonzales, & Jacoby, 1996).

At the same time, when giving a talk at a conference, scientists usually use more explicit forms of talk, even if they end up saying (or reading) things they realize almost everyone in the audience could have inferred based on shared knowledge. They do this as a sign of their status and as a sign of deference to the status of their colleagues and their shared field.

Because of these connections to solidarity and status (deference), many interesting situations can arise. For example, my wife is an academic with me in the same department. When I am speaking to her in a committee meeting—say, responding to something she said—should I talk to her as my wife in the language of solidarity (high-context, inexplicit) or as a fellow professor in the language of status and deference (low-context, explicit)? Usually we opt for the latter choice, but we can slip at times.

We talked in the preceding chapter about adults, regardless of their educational level, talking to children about experience, and not just talking about the "here and now" or giving orders, reprimands, and instructions. Talk about experience is good for children because it is both a type of vicarious experience and a way for adults to model how to think about—and what to focus on in—an experience.

Extended and interactive talk about experience with children requires the adult to be more explicit and to trade less on context. This is so because the child shares less background knowledge about what the adult is talking about, since the adult and child are not talking about the here and now (where there is a clear and mutually visible context). It is also often the case that the child will have little background knowledge about what the adult is talking about, being newer to the world. Such more explicit language, even in the vernacular, requires the adult to model, to some extent, more complex words and patterns of grammar and meaning-making of the sort that children will see in school and especially in more academic styles of talk and writing at school.

For children who have heard too little low-context, explicit forms of talk at home, for whatever reason, schools must allow the child to hear and practice such talk in the vernacular (at first). Furthermore, teachers must make clear to the child that such talk requires the speaker to be explicit and rely less on shared context and background knowledge than is typically the case in everyday talk and interaction. This type of talk is also preparation for school-based forms of literacy, since it is talk that has some of the properties of such writing, for example, staying on one topic, developing the topic coherently and explicitly, and trading more on words and less on context and shared knowledge.

In explicit talk, the child must put into words things that would otherwise be clear from the context. For example, if a child is speaking to other children at school, he or she can say, "I made this," and hold up a candle. But in a report about candle-making, for an absent audience, the child must say something like "I made a candle yesterday" and go on to clearly describe it for someone not looking at it. Even when children are giving a report to their fellow students at school, they must, in such talk, ignore their physical presence and shared knowledge based on personal relationships to a large extent. This is a convention that needs to be learned. It isn't "natural."

Some teachers use an exercise like "sharing time" or "show-and-tell time" to get children to practice more explicit forms of talk as early preparation for literacy. But this can be misleading for some children. Since they can see their friends and classmates in front of them, they are tempted to rely on context and shared knowledge and use high-context, less explicit language. They may even think it would be stupid or rude not to (Michaels, 1981).

However, I have found, working in schools, that children can readily understand a clear rule that says, "Talk like this is being recorded so your Aunt Mary can listen to it later. She is not here now. Assume, too, she knows nothing about candle-making. So be sure she can understand the tape when she listens to it later." The children see this as a game and can readily begin to coach one another when they rely too heavily on shared context by saying things like "Aunt Mary would not have understood that."

We found that even some middle school and high school students need to be told these rules of the game, but they readily catch on. Leaving the rules to tacit knowledge only advantages the students who learned them at home. And, too, we will see below that some cultural groups of people find low-context, explicit language strange and even counter to their cultural practices.

TREATING PEOPLE AS TYPES

Much writing—though not all (e.g., in personal letters and some chat rooms)—tends to be in more explicit (low-context) language. In many highly explicit forms of writing (e.g., essays, editorials, research reports) and talking (e.g., lecturing, reporting, explaining, explicating)—usually in specialist varieties of language—the speaker or writer addresses the listener or reader not as a friend or known person (even if that person is), but as an "audience" made up of types of people for whom the message is intended.

For example, an editorial might be addressed to people in their role as citizens; a report on pollution might be addressed to environmental activists; an essay on video games might be addressed to people as gamers; a recipe is addressed to people as cooks; an explanation of the Electoral College might be addressed to students studying civics. The point is that when we write we often have to think of those we are addressing in terms of some public role, interest, or identity and not in terms of our personal relationships. We have to think of who we are addressing as an audience.

The people whom an essay writer or a lecturer is addressing are, in a sense, "fictions" (Scollon & Scollon, 1981). The people addressed are not treated as people the writer or speaker knows personally, even if they do. They are treated as "rational minds" engaged as types of people who are assumed to have certain types of special interests or knowledge.

In turn, the speaker or writer speaks or writes not as a known individual, not as "Joe" or "Sue," but as a type as well. The speaker or writer is not communicating as an individual private person, but in his or her more public role as an academic, expert, researcher, reporter, advocate, gamer, politician, educator, entertainer, or artist, and so on.

When a child at school gives a report (orally or in writing) on a project, this report is often supposed to be an "academic" exercise. It is supposed to be in more explicit, low-context language. But as we said above, for some children it is odd, even rude, to talk or write to other children and teachers, whom they know well, not as individuals, but as an audience and as types of people. They find it odd that they are supposed to ignore and not make use of the shared personal knowledge and backgrounds of those to whom they are communicating, whom they know well, and whom they sometimes even see right in front of them.

Furthermore, many children writing in school often do not know—and have not been taught—what it means to write as a type of writer (e.g., a researcher, a reporter, an essayist, a literary artist, or an expert on something) and not just as "Johnnie" or "Janie." They do not know what it means to adopt a "voice" as an "author" and not just as their everyday selves. They do not know what it means to write for "strangers" whose specific interests and background knowledge they have to imagine.

Speakers and writers of things like essays and reports can only reply with the shared knowledge—and use this knowledge to let listeners or readers draw inferences—that the types of people they are addressing are all supposed to have (e.g., a writer of a game review can assume gamers all know what a PS4 or a FPS is). It is difficult for a student who is not really in the group of people he or she is supposed to be addressing (e.g., scientists) to make judgments about what everyone in that group can be taken to know and take for granted.

There are cultures—for example, some Native American cultures, but others as well—that highly resist engaging in explicit, low-context talk and writing. In these cultures, people tend to want to communicate only with people they know or whom they have gotten to know by a process of first using talk to explore what is common in their backgrounds. With strangers, people in these cultures tend to stay silent or resist any more than necessary utilitarian talk (Scollon & Scollon, 1981; Wieder & Pratt, 1990).

People in these cultures—and a good many other Americans are in them, besides Native Americans—find explicit, low-context talk and writing (e.g., essays) strange. They are being asked to communicate with people they do not know or with whom they have not become familiar or, worse, to treat people they actually know as types, not individuals. In such contexts, their preference is not to communicate. As Ron Scollon and Suzann Scollon (1981) argued long ago, for such people, things like essays are a form of "cross-cultural" communication for which they may be unprepared.

There is lots of research that shows that more educated parents tend to introduce their children to more explicit, low-context forms of talk and writing both earlier and more copiously at home than do other families (Heath, 1983; Neuman & Celano, 2012; Ochs, Shohet, Campos, & Beck, 2010). For example, they ask even quite young children at dinnertime to report on their day. They encourage a child to be explicit about things that the child knows the parent could readily infer from shared knowledge. The parent is treated as a "stranger" (as the "audience") in a sense and not as a unique person whom the child knows well.

A good many children who have not engaged in lots of explicit, low-context forms of talk at home find the request to be highly explicit in talk, and later in writing, rather strange. Too often teachers ignore this fact or do not know it.

Our first human home is in the forms of high-context talk that are the very basis of living, sharing, and participating with friends, peers, family, and communities. School is, for many, initially a foreign country. It stays that way for far too many students.

Different sorts of literacy practices—such as writing essays, writing scientific reports, interacting in writing conferences, or writing so-called game FAQs (video game strategy guides) out of school—need to be taught and learned as embedded in different (special-interest) "cultures," none of which is no one's first or native culture. These practices are different "ways with words" from people's vernaculars, and they are owned and operated by groups well beyond friends and family.

It is interesting to note that young gamers often write, as referred to above, elaborate and quite technical video game strategy guides (game FAQs) to help other players play a given game. They put these guides up on sites like gamefaqs.com. Such guides are written in a characteristic technical style of language and organized in standard ways.

How do young people learn this new literacy practice? Certainly not at home from their parents and not at school from their teachers. They learn it by participating in the practice with others, but also with teaching, mentoring, models, and feedback from more advanced peers in their "new culture," a "culture" they badly want to enter as a productive member, the culture of gamers and game FAQs.

We can learn some things about how to teach academic language and literacy practices in school from these out-of-school interest-driven cultures that use their own specialist styles of language. This is something we will take up later in this book.

It has always surprised me that while a good many people's success in society—whether at work, as advocates, or in their special interests in life—resides primarily in their oral skills, we pay very little attention to oral skills in school. Teachers should pay attention to types of talk, to their connections to writing, and to how they are used for various functions in society.

Identity and Activity

SAYING AND DOING

Speaking and writing are not just ways to give other people information. They are also forms of action. When we *say* something we almost always intend also to *do* something (Duranti, 1992; Goffman, 1981; Gumperz, 1982; Hanks, 1996). Here are some actions we can carry out through the use of language: greet, inform, insult, encourage, persuade, request, report, describe, explain, propose marriage, question, emote, beg, suggest, bond, show deference, manipulate, support, clarify, lie, promise, flirt, undermine, comfort, advise, correct, order, castigate, entertain, joke, and on and on. Even when we are informing, we are informing for a reason, with purposes and goals.

Actions, whether carried out through language or without it, are often also activities (or what some scholars call *practices*). When a pitcher in a baseball game throws the ball toward home plate from the pitcher's mound, the pitcher is engaging in an action. But pitching is also an activity that is done in similar (but not identical) ways repeatedly and is regulated (in terms of how, where, when, and why it is done) by groups and institutions, namely, baseball leagues and the sport of baseball (Hacking, 2001).

So, too, for many actions done with language. Giving a lecture is an action; lecturing is an activity. Making a request is an action; requesting is an activity that works differently among different social groups and cultures (in terms of what requests you can make to whom, how you need to make them, and how politeness works).

Children learn their first language in the context of action, interaction, and activity. They see language being used to do things and learn to do these things themselves. They don't first have grammar lessons and then later on see what happens when they put language to use in interaction with others. Oddly, though, that is often how language is taught in school.

I now want to talk about both speaking and writing without having to continually use both terms. So I will talk about speaking, but the reader should understand that what I say about speaking here applies to writing as well.

When you speak, you have to know and be able to do three things. First, you have to know what you want to *do* and then be able to craft or design what you say to get it done. This means picking and using an appropriate variety of language to say and do what you want to, a variety that can function to get the job done (Bazerman, 1989). Let's call this *action design* (using language to design and carry out an action, which may well also be an activity).

The second thing you have to know is *who* you want to be taken as when you speak and then to be able to craft or design what you say to come across as enacting that particular identity. All of us have many different identities and can speak out of any one of these or some combination of them (Carbaugh, 1996; Gee, 1990/2015b, 2015a). For example, one and the same person could, in different encounters, speak and act as an everyday person, a friend, a husband or wife, a parent, an African American, a gay person, a linguistics professor, a birder, a gamer, a liberal activist, and much else. Let's call this *speaker/writer design* (using language to design how you want your audience to see you in terms of identity).

The third thing you have to know when you speak is *who* you want your listener(s) to be, what identity you want them to take on when they listen to you. You have to design what you say with your audience in mind, so that your words work to accomplish the action you intend to take.

You must design your language to invite your listener to hear what you say and interpret it from the perspective of a particular identity that listener can take on. A doctor could speak to patients as passive recipients of his or her advice or as proactive advocates for their own health. A politician could address his or her audience as Democratic partisans or as fellow citizens. A teacher could address a student as a special needs student with a label, as just a student, or as a member of a specific community outside school (e.g., as a Mexican American). We will call this *recipient design* (using language to design how you want your audience to respond to you in terms taking on a certain identity; see Sacks & Schegloff, 1974).

Speakers craft what they say to help the listener answer three questions: What is the speaker trying to do? What identity is the speaker speaking from? What identity does the speaker want me to adopt as I listen?

There is a fourth question listeners must answer, and it is this: Do I want to be a compliant listener (and answer the three questions above the way the speaker wants me to), or a resistant listener (and critically question the intentions of the speaker)? Listeners do not have to "behave," though in face-to-face interaction, it is often impolite not to do so. But, of course, resistant listening and reading are often important if we are not to believe everything we hear and read. However, it is often the case that the best way to be resistant and critical is to first listen or read compliantly so that you actually understand what was intended before you critique it.

LANGUAGE AWARENESS

It is impossible to listen if you cannot make out who the speaker takes you to be and what he or she wants to do. However, listeners have to be wary of misleading language, language that claims to be doing one thing to one sort of audience but actually is doing something else to another type of audience. Misleading language seems to be everywhere these days.

Consider, as an example, the text below from a famous psychological experiment:

> The procedure is actually quite simple. First you arrange things into different groups. Of course, one pile may be sufficient depending on how much there is to do. If you have to go somewhere else due to lack of facilities that is the next step, otherwise you are pretty well set. It is important not to overdo things. That is, it is better to do too few things at once than too many. In the short run this may not seem important but complications can easily arise. A mistake can be expensive as well. At first the whole procedure will seem complicated.
>
> Soon, however, it will become just another facet of life. It is difficult to foresee any end to the necessity for this task in the immediate future, but then one never can tell. After the procedure is completed one arranges the materials into different groups again. Then they can be put into their appropriate places. Eventually they will be used once more and the whole cycle will then have to be repeated. However, that is part of life. (Bransford, & Johnson, 1972, p. 722)

When people were asked to read this passage, it made no sense to them and they could remember next to none of it later. When you read this now, chances are good you have no idea what the author is trying to do, though you know what is being said. When the subjects in the experiment were told that the text was describing doing laundry, it then made sense and they could remember it much better later.

What the experimenters did not say, however, is that when you do know what the text is about—doing laundry—you readily realize that this text was not very well designed to tell someone how to do laundry. It is hard, indeed, to know whom this text could really have been meant for as an audience, except subjects in a psych experiment (certainly not people in need of help doing their laundry).

This experiment was meant to show that people cannot understand texts unless they know what they are about. But this experiment also shows, inadvertently, that we all realize that the text is really an attempt to manipulate experimental subjects (get them to experience a sense of not understanding and being confused) in a psych experiment. The text is, in reality, designed for recipients who are meant to get confused in a psych experiment. And for this it is well designed. It is just not well designed to tell someone how to do laundry. Thus, once we know the text is about laundry we understand it better in one way, but we are still confused why anyone would describe doing laundry this way. We can see that it is not language that fits well with the action it was (supposedly) meant to accomplish.

Many students in school are situated much as are subjects in the laundry text experiment. When given a text, too often they do not know what it is meant to do and even if they are told what it is meant to do, they do not know if it is well designed or not to achieve its aims. This is so because in school we do not teach language and literacy in the context of actions in the world. To know how to pull off an action with language or with any other tool—say a football or a baseball—one has to practice in the contexts (on the sorts of fields) where the "game" is played. Actions do not just happen out of any context. And in any context in which they happen, lots more is going on than just the action itself.

Students often have a right to be befuddled. Often a text claims it is meant to do one thing but it is actually meant to do another. It is not well designed for what it *claims* to be doing but is well designed for what it is *actually* doing. Many textbooks, for example, claim they are about informing students, and informing is an act that is meant to produce understanding. In reality, research shows that textbooks are usually poorly written (designed) for understanding. They are written for coverage.

Publishers know that many a textbook has failed to sell well because it did not cover something some teacher or policymaker wanted, but few have failed because they covered too much. Additionally, educational boards and policymakers mandate what should be covered, and it is most often far too much for any deep understanding. The textbook solution is to say a little about a lot when understanding is better accomplished by saying a lot about a little (that is, staying on a topic for a while).

In reality, the language in many textbooks is designed for an audience made up of teachers, policymakers, and, in some cases, politically motivated activists who want to see some things covered in the "right" way and other things left out. Textbooks are also often designed to address students not as real learners but as test-takers. It is not surprising that research has shown that textbooks are an ineffective educational tool, though this has not stopped us from using them (Graesser et al., 2004).

On many reading tests students face passages that seem to be stories but in fact are carefully constructed texts meant to lead to a bell curve distribution of scores on the test. They are not meant to entertain and are designed for students not as readers or people but as score-producers of a certain sort.

Mathematics word problems use everyday narrative details to motivate students to engage in numerical computations that, in actuality, have nothing to do with the narrative details. The student is basically meant to ignore the narrative details as part of any larger narrative or experiential context.

Consider an example of a math word problem:

Lisa invited the entire third grade to her party.
There are 48 students altogether.
23 of the students are boys and 25 are girls.
9 students will not be able to go to the party.
How many students will be there?
(www.mathplayground.com/wpdatabase/
Addition_Subtraction_RGExInfo_3.htm)

What, for heaven's sake, does the fact that there are two more girls than boys in this class have to do with the math problem or anything else, for that matter? If there are 48 kids in the class and 9 aren't coming, then 39 are coming (or intending to). No one needs to know or care about gender distribution in the class. In everyday life, telling people information that is irrelevant and pointless is either rude or deranged.

Indeed, the world is chock-full of texts that seem to be written to do one thing and seem to be written for certain sorts of people but, in reality, are written to do another thing and for another audience. Sometimes language is crafted to speak to two or more disparate audiences at once, as when a politician uses words and phrasings that can be understood differently by racists and nonracists or highly religious people and secular people.

It is important that people learn how to think about language—about speaking, listening, reading, and writing—so that they can critically reflect on what speakers or writers are trying to do, who they take themselves to be, and whom they intend to address (Bizzell, 1992; Gee, 2013). Sometimes, the speaker or writer is not a person but an institution, a group, or a person (e.g., a speechwriter for a politician) speaking or writing in the name of someone else. This capacity to think about communication at a metalevel is sometimes called *language awareness*. There was a time when some British schools actively taught language awareness, but we in the United States rarely have (Fairclough, 1992).

Language awareness allows us to better understand how talk and texts work in the world. It allows us to better understand actors and institutions, whether these be test-makers, politicians, salespeople, or advocates for various causes and viewpoints. There is research showing that children who do not realize that narratives in math problems and on reading tests are not meant to be treated as real stories (where people are meant to make inferences based on their past experiences to fill out the meaning of the story) do poorly on both sorts of tests. And there is ample evidence in the real world that people do not consider carefully enough what politicians and advocates are actually saying and trying to do and whom they are really addressing (Luntz, 2007).

ACTIVITIES IN AN ECOLOGY

I argued above that speaking and writing are forms of action. We pointed out, as well, that a great many actions that we carry out with language are activities (practices). Saying, "I pronounce you man and wife" is action—indeed one carried out primarily by language—but it is also an activity done regularly in typical ways and normed and regulated by the state and various religious institutions.

Actions that are activities are always part of a set of related activities that give meaning to one another (Engeström, 1987; Latour, 2005). Any one activity has a place in the whole set of related activities. Let's call the whole set an *activity ecology*.

Lecturing is an activity that has a place among other academic activities like writing syllabi, leading discussion groups, giving reading assignments, giving writing assignments, writing and grading exams, and granting course credits. Looking up the identity of a bird in a bird guide, for birders, is an activity that has a place among other activities, such as seeing a bird through binoculars, listening to its calls, noting the habitat the bird is in, noting its field marks (its most distinctive features), keeping bird lists, and comparing notes with other birders.

When we study literacy we need to study literacy activities as parts of literacy ecologies. When we teach literacy we need to teach literacy activities as parts of literacy ecologies. A scientific journal article is a literacy activity. It is written in a particular style that is normed and regulated by journals and academic institutions. But it exists in a larger ecology of activities like doing research, giving talks at conferences, holding lab meetings, writing and circulating drafts, reading reviews, doing revisions, and writing grants.

I now want to show that we can understand what a text means and make judgments about it only if we know what activity that text is carrying out and how that activity fits into an ecology of related activities. I could take as an example here an academic article, a news story, an ad, a policy report, a test, or much else as my example. However, I want to use an example that represents a particularly modern type of text, one that is sometimes quite controversial. However, what I say here would apply equally well to any other type of text or talk that exists in an ecology of related activities.

Consider the text below (Gee, 2015a, p. 16):

As u can see I gave my page a little makeover! I've had that old one for over a year! Needed a change! As 4 LH 1.3 I've got around thirty slides, working up to my usual 127! Patience is all it takes! I garentee it'll B out B4 Xmas though! ;)

    <3 A

Language like this gives rise to great consternation on the part of many adults. Some of them even wonder if such things betoken the death of written language as we know (knew) it. The spelling errors and unedited typos bother some people to no end.

However, it is crucial to realize that no one can conclude anything about this text and its language unless he or she knows how it is embedded in a whole set of related activities in which it lives. Any text exists within an *ecology* of activities and can be fully understood and judged only within that ecology and the role it plays there.

So let's see where this text lives and where it gets its significance from. It was written by a 15-year-old girl named Alex who plays the video game *The Sims* and uses images from the game to write vampire romance fan fiction.

The Sims series of video games are the best-selling video games in history. In *The Sims,* players (over half of whom are girls and women) design, build, and maintain families, neighborhoods, and communities. *The Sims* is a life and family simulator.

Some players do not just play *The Sims*; they also use it to write a form of graphic fan fiction. In their most basic form, *Sims* fan fiction stories are created by taking screenshots during *Sims* game play, which are then sometimes transformed by using tools like Photoshop. Players write words to accompany the screenshots, words that take the form of a continuous narrative across many pages of images and words. The writer has to produce a multimodal (words and images) text using digital tools (the game; graphic design tools to modify the images; and sites for posting, reviewing, and critiquing stories).

Alex is a very popular *Sims* vampire romance fan fiction writer who has thousands of loyal and admiring readers. She writes her stories for her fellow teenagers on an interest-driven Internet site devoted to *Sims* fan fiction. Below is what one teen has to say about Alex's *Lincoln Heights* series of stories. It is clear that for this teen, Alex's writing is helpful in a deep way. (This quote is from the discussion thread on *Lincoln Heights* at The Sims Writers' Hangout.)

i LOVELOVELOVE Lincoln Heights. When i read it always seems to cure my sadness and it has actually helped me deal with alot of depression and shit i've been forced to deal with lately. I can't wait until the next chapter is out... HURRY UP, ALEX!
xo. :]

When Alex started writing stories on the site, she spelled poorly, her writing was weak, and she came close to plagiarizing the famous *Twilight* books. School had done little for her in the way of literacy. Others on the site made it clear to her that posted stories had to be well-written, spelled correctly, well-edited, and original. And they mentored her and helped her. She saw models of good work and received encouragement and critical feedback on her own work. She has now become adept at graphic design and writing. Indeed, some readers tell her they like her stories better than the *Twilight* stories.

Consider, for instance, the beginning of *Lincoln Heights* (minus the images). As the story's description, Alex uses a quote:

Description:
  "You cannot call it love, for your age the heyday in the blood is tame" —William Shakespeare

Then the actual story begins with (remember each of these sentences has a specially designed image accompanying it):

Devin Collins rolled his dark eyes as his younger sister, Julia, whined about leaving all her little friends in New York.

"I still don't get why 'we' have to move here when it's Ariel's parents who died!"

Devin glared at his sister. She was ten: five years younger than himself, but she knew exactly how to piss him off.

Note here how "whined" and "little friends" are, though in the narrator's voice, actually infected by Devin's voice, as it is he who would think of Julia as whining and her friends as "little." This is a form of indirect quotation that is common in novels. The direct quotation "I still don't get why 'we' have to move here when it's Ariel's parents who died!" is not explicitly attributed to the sister but is clearly understood to be her speaking and, indeed, a representation of her whining. The emphasis on "we" gives the word a stress that sounds like whining.

The introduction of Ariel, a character we do not yet know, starts the story in media res (in the middle) and, again, places the narration inside the private knowledge and minds of Devin and his sister. This creates suspense and forces the reader to wonder who Ariel is. This, too, is a technique common in novels. And, again, "piss him off," though not a direct quote, is a paraphrasing of Devin's language or thoughts. And, of course, "rolled his dark eyes" is a phrasing meant to capture teenage girl readers at the outset (and it does—girls on the thread say Devin is "theirs" and comment on his attractiveness repeatedly). Remember, too, that Alex has designed pictures not only to fit her story but also to appeal deeply to her teen readers. Alex, indeed, knows her readers very well.

Alex posts regular updates on her blog and on the Sims Writers' Hangout thread to keep her fans informed about progress on upcoming chapters, as well as other things about her life and writing. The text we started with—the one that offends so many adults—is one of these posts:

> As u can see I gave my page a little makeover! I've had that old one for over a year! Needed a change! As 4 LH 1.3 I've got around thirty slides, working up to my usual 127! Patience is all it takes! I garentee it'll B out B4 Xmas though! ;)
> <3 A

Alex is enacting the identity of a *Sims* fan fiction writer of vampire romance. This is *who* she writing as. This is an identity her teen readers readily recognize.

This identity involves engaging in activities (like posting) that are part of the larger overall ecology of *Sims* fan fiction writing activities. This larger ecology involves, among others, such activities as the following:

Using in-game design tools as well as various other design tools such as Adobe Photoshop.

Creating and maintaining a personal website through which Alex energizes her fan base.

Keeping her fans updated on her activities and responding to them via various type of social media.

Writing fan fiction in a very specific graphic and narrative genre.

Working with fans who help her edit her work

Designing images and matching them to text (multimodality literacy).

Using the appropriate style of language for different activities.

Note that the post we saw earlier from Alex—the one that bothers some people for its errors and informality—plays a specific role in the ecology of what Alex is doing and who she is being when she is being a *Sims* fan fiction writer. It is a way to bond with her teen readers and to motivate them to be devoted readers and followers (her fans). Its language is meant to function in these terms and does so very well indeed.

Note that Alex writes quite differently when she composes her stories. Here she edits them (with help from some of her most devoted readers who volunteer to be editors), and they are free of errors. This is because this form of writing plays a different role in the larger ecology of who Alex is being and what she is doing.

When anyone gets good at an ecology of related activities, he or she picks up certain skills. One way to look at the problem of transfer is to ask, What other skills are being acquired here and how can they prepare a person to learn in the future? What other activity ecologies are they a good preparation for?

Alex learned each activity in her activity ecology as part of the whole system, not in isolation. She learned the whole system via participation in a distributed teaching and learning system where others mentored her, resourced her, encouraged her, and became her audience (as she is sometimes theirs). This, I believe, has important implications for how we can teach people literacy activities in and out of school. It has implications, as well, for the different sorts of skills young people can acquire and where they can get these skills.

CHAPTER 7

Identities

KNOWING, DOING, BEING

Think a moment about mimes (yes, mimes). A person could know about mimes, even know a lot about them, but not be able to do any miming. And, then, too, a person could be able to do some miming, play around a bit, but not actually be a mime. Knowing, doing, and being (being something like a mime) are different things.

What does it mean to *be* a mime? It means that a person identifies as a mime. The person is "into it." It means, as well, that the person is accepted as a mime, not just by non-mimes but also by other committed and respected mimes. The person might, indeed, sometimes be referred to by others as a "real mime." When someone is a mime in this way I will say they have a "mime identity" (that is, they identify themselves as mimes, and also others, including other mimes, identify them or recognize them as mimes). This, of course, involves a special use of the word *identity*, a word that is used in many different ways.

School is usually about knowing. Imagine that miming was a school "subject" (like physics or mathematics). Students would primarily be taught information about mimes and miming and then tested on their retention of this information.

As we said, knowing about miming, even knowing a lot about miming, does not mean that a person could actually do any miming. That would require practice, lots of it. Knowledge about something does not readily translate into an ability to do it. For example, research has shown that many students who "know" Newton's laws of motion (i.e., can write them down on a test) cannot use them to solve problems in physics, even problems whose solutions can be deduced logically from Newton's laws (Chi, Feltovich, & Glaser, 1981).

JUDGMENT SYSTEMS

Doing, rather than just *knowing*, is important. If we cannot do, then we cannot function in the world and solve problems. However, doing, especially at school, though elsewhere as well, faces an interesting, but rarely discussed, problem. The problem is what I will call "the missing judgment system."

Newcomers need, but do not have, what I will call a *judgment system* for the activity in which they want to engage (Gee, 2004, 2015a; Schön, 1983). A judgment system tells people engaged in a particular activity or domain of activity what constitutes a good choice about where and how to start, how to judge which outcomes from their actions are good or not for their goals or purposes, and what some good things to do next are if your actions are not succeeding. What I am calling a judgment system could also be called an "assessment system" or an "appreciative system" (ways of appreciating choices and outcomes for what they are worth).

When people are first learning to do anything complicated they have to try things out and see what happens. Since they are beginners, they do not necessarily know what a good thing to try first is. And they don't know what a good thing to try next is if the first attempt does not work or work well enough. Indeed, they may not even know what counts as "working" or "working well enough."

So how do newcomers (learners) learn what is a good thing to try? How do they learn to evaluate what happens (the result of their action) when they try something? How do they know whether the result was good, bad, or indifferent for their goal? How do they learn, when what they try does not work out, what to do next? Obviously, they cannot act if they have no answers to these questions. They would be at a loss. Simple trial and error, with no guidance, is ineffective at best and, in learning complex things, it is unlikely to work.

Imagine I am planting a food garden for the first time. Should I start from seeds or already started plants? When and where is the best place to plant which plants? What should be in—or what should I put in—the dirt? What do I do about insects, gophers, and wild animals like deer or javelinas in Arizona, where I live? What does a healthy plant look like at various stages of growth? How will I know when my plants are ready to be harvested, something that will differ for each type of plant? When I have a specific problem and what I do to try to solve it does not work, what is a good thing to do next, rather than just flailing around trying anything I can think of? None of this says trial and error is not an important part of the process of learning. What it says is that trial and error usually needs to be part of a larger process of mentorship and socialization into a specific social group's activities.

These are just a few of the questions a newcomer faces. Now, where could a learner of gardening, miming, or physics get (learn) a judgment system for gardening, miming, or physics? Who determines what good, useful expectations, norms, values, and choices are in a domain like gardening, miming, or physics? Who determines what a successful action or one in need of redoing is? Who determines, if things have not worked out, what a good thing to do next is, rather than just giving up?

It is the people who *are* gardeners, mimes, or physicists who determine this. It is their values, norms, and ways of "going on" from one attempt to another in a path past failure to success that constitute the judgment system for the domain. It is the people who are into it and have earned the respect of others who are into it. Of course, these people cannot just give a judgment system full-blown to newcomers. It takes mentorship, time, and practice to develop it in a newcomer.

And, of course, newcomers do need to be encouraged to try things out and see what happens (remember horizontal learning and mucking around), but this means lowering the cost of failure so that they can explore and take risks without dire consequences. That is part of teaching and mentorship as well.

So how do students in school develop the judgment systems they need for engaging in successful action? Whether students in school are learning miming or physics, most of them will never become "real" mimes or physicists. And yet the learner can't really do miming or physics without having begun the course of internalizing the judgment system of real mimes or physicists. The best way to do this would be to begin the process of actually becoming a mime or a physicist with real mimes or physicists. But this is not very realistic in most cases of schooling.

So schools face a deep problem if they want to focus on doing and not just knowing. The problem is that very often the judgment systems (connected to being) that help and guide people on what to do, why to do it, and how to do it well in a given domain are missing. They are missing because the "real" mimes, physicists, or whatever are not there.

This problem—the problem of missing judgment systems—helps explain why schools keep falling back on knowing and not doing and being. It helps explain, too, why so much doing in school (in labs and projects, for example) does not lead to deep knowledge that can be put to use out of school and for a lifetime. Too often no authentic judgment systems are at play, only, at best, made-up and contrived ones.

Below I will discuss how people get authentic judgment systems out of school, even people who are not intending to go all the way to being a "real X" (e.g., a real mime, a real physicist), as is so often the case in school. But first, let me say that there is, of course, a role for knowing facts and information. There are a great many things people need to know in order to participate with understanding in their society. Furthermore, knowing facts and information in a given domain is a sine qua non for being able to understand talk and texts in that domain, especially specialist low-context talk and texts. So I do not want to denigrate facts and information.

However, while some facts and information must just be taught, there are lots of important facts and information that can be used by learners and experts as tools for solving problems. Here there is no need to drill students on facts and information out of the context of problem solving. Indeed, as students use facts and information repeatedly to solve problems and argue the case for their solutions, they will have used and rehearsed the facts and information so often they will not only know these facts; they will also have organized them into a well-integrated knowledge system that can fuel problem solving and innovation (Shaffer, 2007). Very often, doing is the best way to gain knowledge, since you repeatedly have to put the knowledge to meaningful use.

But we still face the problem that there is no doing without being, and therefore learners who are learning to do, and not just know, need access to the judgment systems of real mimes or physicists or whatever "real X" sets the standards, norms, values, and ways of proceeding in the domain to be learned.

GETTING JUDGMENT SYSTEMS OUTSIDE SCHOOL

So what could schools do about missing judgment systems? Well, they could ensure that every miming class is taught by a real mime and every physics class is taught by a real physicist. What *real* means here is that the teacher has internalized the judgment system of a mime or physicist and, in that sense, *is* a mime or a physicist. Such teachers do not need a formal credential (e.g., a PhD); they need a recognizable identity as a mime or physicist.

Supplying at every level of schooling a real X (a real mime, a real physicist, a real artist, a real biologist, and so forth) for every X that students study in school is a nonstarter, at least given our current schools and teacher-training programs. To allow every student access to mentorship from a real X for any X they study would certainly require radical paradigm change in our schools and schools of education.

So let's look at how people acquire judgment systems out of school and what this might imply for paradigm change in schools. In cases like gardening or cooking, newcomers get a judgment system by being mentored and socialized into gardening or cooking by families and communities where there are more senior and adept gardeners and cooks around.

Another classic case of passing on judgment systems is when graduate students are apprenticed to a laboratory. Professors and more advanced peers incorporate the graduate student into ongoing, often collaborative, talk, instruction, practice, and problem solving. In the process, over time, the graduate student internalizes the judgment system of the lab and knows how to start, do, redo, and evaluate outcomes. The graduate student has internalized a set of norms, values, and "ways of going on" (what to do next).

Another situation in which judgment systems are passed is in good parenting. Parents (and more advanced peers) in a family incorporate the young child into activities that the child cannot yet do alone. In the process, through talk, modeling, guidance, and shared action, the parent-child team pulls off a successful action (with possibly several attempts before success). In the process the child is internalizing the norms, values, attitudes, and ways of going on in various sorts of activities that will make the child "one of us," a member of this family, committed to doing things "our" way.

DISTRIBUTED TEACHING AND LEARNING SYSTEMS

Today there are new places—pregnant with possibilities for paradigm change in teaching and learning in and out of school—where people experience authentic judgment systems, whether they want to go all the way to being a real X or just learn something about what it means to be an X. Indeed, these new places speak so well to how to teach knowing, doing, and being (and not just knowing) that they constitute a new and more modern out-of-school school system.

Today, when young people have an interest in something and want to take it further, they can join interest-driven collaborative groups, often on the Internet, but sometimes in the physical world as well (Ito et al., 2013). These digital or physical sites offer all sorts of instruction, mentoring, coaching, guidance, and modeling, all of which incorporate the norms and values (the judgment system) of people who have carried the interest that drives the group over into a passion (an identity, a way of being).

Take as one example gamers who play the game *DOTA 2* (Holmes, 2016). *DOTA 2* is a very complex team-based game of action and strategy. Players must know how to choose heroes to play from a pool of well over a hundred heroes and then form two teams of five players each. Each hero has different skills and those skills can be leveled up (improved) in different ways as the player gains experience and success in the game. *DOTA 2* requires players to make myriad complicated and often technical choices, but help is available. Here is what one interest-driven website has to say to newcomers:

> So many choices: How can I stay in the fight longer? Which ability will bring my foe to their knees? Do these boots match my Divine Rapier? Even the greatest warrior needs a mentor—let your fellow players help you learn the finer points of strategy with Guides and Hero Builds.
>
> By visiting the "Guides" section in the Steam Community, you can now view in-depth walkthroughs of all your favorite heroes. You can also subscribe to Hero Builds, which can be used in-game to instruct you on what abilities to level up (and when), along with what items will best suit your needs. (www.dota2.com/workshop/builds/overview)

Players who want to get good at *DOTA 2*—ones whose interest is strong—can go to a large number of different websites, many of them designed by the players themselves, to gain teaching of all different sorts. This is not just informal learning; it is informal teaching. Players can even customize how they want to be taught.

There are sites with all sorts of different strategy guides, some in text form, some in videos. There are sites where players have designed tutorials for others, some of them examples of quite explicit instruction. There are sites where players can watch others play, with or without annotation or commentary. Players can go to sites where they can get a coach that will actually enter their own game and assist them. There are sites—like the one we just quoted—that offer advice for building up (leveling up) the skills of a hero and teach players how to think about and evaluate different choices. There are sites where players work together to "theory craft"; that is, they seek to figure out the complicated and often hidden statistical models that underlie the game and, in turn, to figure out how to make effective use of these statistics or even redesign them for better and fairer play. And there are all sorts of different forums where players can discuss the game, ask questions, share information, make suggestions, and debate different values and strategies.

This large set of related *DOTA 2* sites I will call, following Holmes (2016), a *distributed teaching and learning system* (Hayes & Gee, in press). Across the sites, master players and more senior players guide, instruct, and collaborate with newer players. The new players, in the process, internalize the judgment system of "real *DOTA 2*" players. Better yet, players can teach and mentor what they are good at; learn from others what they are not yet good at; and seek new, higher challenges to their expertise by "upping their game" through new learning and new styles of play.

The *DOTA 2* distributed system of teaching and learning is but one example. Today you can hardly pick a topic that does not offer such a system. People engage in this sort of interest-and-passion-fueled teaching and learning on topics like media production, women's health, citizen science, political activism, game design, fan fiction writing, robotics, pet care, and almost anything else you can imagine (including, on the "dark web," how to do identity theft or be a "real jihadist").

People enter such distributed teaching and learning systems because of an interest. They are led in the development of skills, norms, and values by those who have a passion for the domain and who have put in a great many hours of deliberate practice. Newcomers can, if they choose, remain long enough just to hone their interest or to realize they are not motivated to take the interest much further. Or they can fuel their interest so it becomes a passion, stay a lot longer, and become a real X who teaches/mentors what they authentically know how to do and evaluate.

In any case, even newcomers who choose not to go all the way to passion have experienced up close and personally the judgment system of the domain and can understand and appreciate what the domain does, means, and values and why. And that is good and important learning on its own. Indeed, I would argue that young people should be mentored to sample lots of different interests and encouraged to find one or more interest to become a passion that fuels deep skills, values, and affiliation with others who have achieved mastery.

THE ZONE OF PROXIMAL DEVELOPMENT

All the examples of overcoming the missing-judgment-system paradox—socialization within families and communities, parenting, laboratories, and distributed teaching and learning systems—are examples of what Vygotsky (1978) called learning within the zone of proximal development (the ZPD). Liberal educators have interpreted Vygotsky in ways he would not have recognized. The ZPD is not necessarily a "warm and fuzzy" place (Wertsch, 1985).

For Vygotsky, a child's ZPD contains the skills that are almost ready to "hatch." They are the skills where if children can get help from an adult to pull them off together collaboratively, the children will thereby soon learn how to do them by themselves. In the ZPD, adults cooperate with children (or "masters" cooperate with "apprentices") to carry out some action the children cannot yet do on their own. In the process, adults impose their interpretations, values, and norms onto the child by modeling and using them—and sometimes overtly talking about then—in the cooperative action. This is what I have called a *judgment system*.

In time, children internalize the adult's judgment system, and when they can eventually carry out the action on their own, they do so with the adult's judgment system in mind, usually unconsciously. This is also what is going on as newcomers enter distributed teaching and learning sites. They internalize the interpretations, values, and norms of the real Xs in the domain; in the *DOTA 2* case, these would be the "real *DOTA 2* players." It is what goes on in laboratories. Graduate students internalize the interpretations, values, and norms of real physicists of not just any old type, but of the type in their lab.

The ZPD is a form of socialization or colonization, depending on how you view the norms and values being internalized. There is no way out of socialization or colonization, at least for young people and newcomers. It is their best access to the judgment systems they need for successful action in a domain. Someone who passionately wants to be a real *DOTA 2* player wants to be "colonized" by the real *DOTA 2* players. They are the people who can grant the person access to the "inside" of the team, group, community, domain, or whatever we want to call it.

This does not mean that learners must stop with and never develop new or transformed judgment systems. But that ability comes from metaknowledge about the judgment system. Such metaknowledge is gained through explicit talk with others and through the overt explication, comparison, contrast, and testing of different perspectives. Many a truly talented real X has such metaknowledge and uses it to introduce innovation, transformation, and change into the domain.

The act of socializing or colonizing (take your pick) becomes problematic when learners are not allowed access to metaknowledge about perspectives and judgment systems in the domain and in related domains. This happens when parents, professors, teachers, or mentors don't eventually (when the learner has achieved enough mastery of the "standards") talk about, defend, critically discuss, and openly reflect on their vales and norms with learners. It happens when they don't eventually talk about and critically assess the role, for good or ill, or a bit of both, that their domain has played or does play in the world. Minus such overt and reflective critical discussion, socialization truly turns into colonization.

SCHOOL

In its classic version, Vygotsky's zone of proximal development is a realm where social interaction between a mentor/teacher (who could be a parent, or a *DOTA2* master, of course) and a learner takes place. This type of one-on-one cooperative action where the mentor/teacher scaffolds the performance and thinking of the learner is rare in school. Teachers usually face too many students at too many different levels (with, that is, very different ZPDs). However, what we have been calling distributed teaching and learning systems have created a new "group" version of learning within the ZPD.

In a distributed teaching and learning system there need not be, and rarely is, one mentor/teacher. Rather, for different activities and skills there are different people to serve as mentors/teachers; there are different places to go; and there are different sorts of tools, technologies, and media to act as surrogate mentors/teachers. The distributed system is a hive of connected activities. Learners at all different levels can traverse this hive and dive into the places that have mentors and tools that are right for their current ZPD for a given skill.

A distributed teaching and learning system is a self-organizing one in which people can pair up with the right other people and the right tools at the right time for ZPD learning. This means being able to find the help you need so you can do together with a mentor what you will, with that help, soon be able to do alone. As you engage with different sorts of help across the system over time, you are internalizing the judgment system for the interest/passion that drives the distributed teaching and learning system. You may internalize it so far that you become a real X or just far enough to accomplish what you need to learn to do for the purposes you have.

By the way, I should note that there are important things to learn to do that we never learn all by ourselves and shouldn't. There are today a good many problem-solving activities that require collaboration and collective intelligence (Brown & Lauder, 2000; Levy, 1999; Nielsen, 2012). This means we all have to learn how to be part of an intelligent team and not just someone who goes it alone. Schools, of course, barely touch on collaboration and collective intelligence, save to view them with suspicion as possible forms of cheating. Today we need to think of the ZPD and learning in the ZPD as it applies to a team and not just a person. This problem has barely been touched on, but literature on team-based ZPDs is beginning to grow (e.g., Aguilar, 2016).

There are already distributed teaching and learning systems devoted to interests that are "school-like," such interests as types of media design, tech skills, citizen science, history, mythology, social issues and activism, and all sorts of creative activity. But such systems are a very different paradigm from that of school as we know it. Schools are institutions and, as such, they are subject to all the ills of institutions. Distributed teaching and learning systems are usually self-organizing systems in no need of formal institutions for their support.

Distributed teaching and learning systems are making teaching ubiquitous today. Teaching is no longer restricted to schools and classrooms. It is no longer incorporated into just single individuals. It is distributed across different people and smart tools and technologies. The learning that goes on in distributed teaching and learning systems is neither informal or formal, but something different. It is participatory and immersive, but it involves multiple forms of instruction, some quite didactic.

CHAPTER 8

The Pareto Principle and Identities

THE PARETO PRINCIPLE

In 1941 Joseph Juran, an engineer and management consultant, formulated what he called the Pareto principle (Anderson, 2006; Gee & Hayes, 2010, 2011; Reed, 2001; Shirky, 2008). He named the principle after the Italian economist Vilfredo Pareto, who discovered it in 1896. The principle is sometimes called "the 80–20 rule" or "the law of the vital few." Pareto pointed out that 80% of the land in Italy was owned by 20% of the population and that 20% of the peapods in his garden contained 80% of the peas.

Juran realized that the Pareto principle applies quite widely. The general rule can be stated in several different ways; here is one: For many events or activities, roughly 80% of the effects come from 20% of the causes. On a photo-sharing site, 20% of the people on the site will post 80% of the photos. In sales, 80% of sales come from 20% of the customers. In any academic field, 80% of the publications in the field come from 20% of the academics in the field. In the United States, the top 20% of the population own 80% of the wealth; actually, by 2014 they owned 93% of it. In many cases a Pareto distribution is more skewed than 80–20, as is the case with wealth.

The Pareto principle is actually a "power law. " What this means is that if we take the 20% that contributes 80% of the outcomes, in this top 20% the same 80–20 distribution will hold. In this small group of "major contributors," the top 20% will contribute much more than the bottom 80% of the small group. And so on. In the end, the top 1% contribute (or own), by far and away, the most.

The Pareto principle applies to interest-driven sites where people share with one another and often make things. These are the sites that, when they are networked together around a specific interest, become distributed teaching and learning systems. I argued in the preceding chapter that these systems are competitors to schools in the development of skills, passion, and mastery. On such sites, 20% will share, contribute, or make much more than the other 80% and the top 1% will share, contribute, or make far more than anyone else. This just seems to be how many human activities, and many activities in nature, are organized.

But this is not the way that things are organized at school. School is all about bell curves. In a bell curve there are a small number of people at the top and a small number at the bottom and the vast majority are lumped together in the middle. School is so much about bell curves that when we don't get them, we redesign our tests to ensure that the numbers come out in a bell curve. Yet when humans are let free from testers and policymakers, they often fall into a Pareto distribution in their activities.

There is a common misunderstanding about the 80% who contribute 20% in a Pareto distribution. We might think they are the "losers." They are not. In most human activities where people choose to do it, there are few or no people who don't care enough or do not have the wherewithal to make contributions. Why would people choose the activity otherwise, when they can choose another one?

The bottom 80% are made up of people who join an activity or site to gain resources or help they need and then leave to engage in their "own thing," or they are people who stay longer but contribute at a moderate level. For many members of this latter group, integration into the activity or site is life-enhancing, and often their contributions count and sometimes are deeply important.

People in the 80% have an interest, often a strong one, but not a passion as strong as those who make up the top 20%. Take, as an example, academics. I mentioned above that in any academic area, 20% of the academics in the area publish 80% of the articles and books (and the top 1% publish even a great deal more than anyone else in the top 20%). As things stand, universities make publishing the core and status-giving activity of academics. But there are academics who prefer to teach, read, and write more slowly or outside the mainstream of their field. Academic institutions could not exist without these people. And, once in a while, such people publish something the big contributors have not, and could not, have thought of.

That said, the top 20% in an activity are the dynamic generators of ideas, inventions, products, and knowledge. They are the people who are passionate about what they do, who are into it, who are "gung ho." They are the people who reap the most rewards, whether these be money, status, or respect for doing good for others. We will see, though, that the 80% can be a source of "mutations," skills or knowledge that the top 20% just do not have. This is because, very often, the people in the 80% have had some experiences that people in the 20% have not had.

The world we live in today is full of complexity and is badly in need of people who can solve hard problems. It is a Pareto world, not a bell curve world. What this means is that every young person, in and out of school, should be able to sample lots of interests, take some of these far enough to sample them or contribute moderately to them, and take one or a few far enough to gain a passion and join the top 20%.

By the way, sites where one is in the 80% can be a source of ideas for another site where a person is in the top 20%. To take a personal example: As an academic, I am in the top 20%. I have published a great deal. As a gamer, I am in the 80%, and not all that high up in it. I am, nonetheless, a "real gamer." It turns out that being a gamer has been an important inspiration for some of my most successful academic publications, even ones not directly on games and gaming. Gaming is an activity in which many other academics my age (68, as I write this) have no interest. Some would say—indeed have said—that my gaming interest is trivial or a waste of time. It isn't. By no means do I game in order to further my academic career, but, nonetheless, gaming has changed me as an academic.

WISDOM OF CROWDS

The world today faces a great many serious risks from interacting complex systems like global warming; environmental degradation; massive flows of migrants; a global economy based on numbers flowing through computers; massive inequality; and global conflicts over religion, water, and declining resources. In such a world, credentialed experts, as we traditionally think of them, can be dangerous (Weinberger, 2012).

Traditional experts are people who know a great deal about a narrow subject matter. They tend to underestimate the importance of what they don't know; to apply their methods and tools to problems beyond their scope; and to engage in forms of groupthink as "members" of a sort of intellectual "club."

A good example of narrow single-minded expertise gone dangerously awry is Alan Greenspan. Greenspan served as chair of the Federal Reserve of the United States from 1987 until 2006. He was one of the most respected, and indeed even revered, economists in history. He was a major force behind economic policy in the United States and globally when he headed the Federal Reserve. Nonetheless, his policies directly helped bring on the disastrous 2008 worldwide recession, by far the worst economic collapse since the Great Depression of the 1930s.

When Greenspan was asked by a congressional committee if he thought he had made any mistakes, he said:

> I made a mistake in presuming that the self-interest of organizations, specifically banks and others, were such (as that?) they were best capable of protecting their own shareholders and their equity in the firms. And it's been my experience, having worked both as a regulator for 18 years and similar quantities in the private sector, especially 10 years at a major international bank, that the loan officers of those institutions knew far more about the risks involved in the people to whom they lent money than I saw even our best regulators at the Fed capable of doing.
>
> So the problem here is, something which looked to be a very solid edifice, and indeed a critical pillar to market competition and free markets, did break down. And I think that, as I said, shocked me.
>
> I still do not fully understand why it happened. (law.du.edu/documents/corporate-governance/legislation/preliminary-transcript-crisis.pdf, parentheses in original)

Here is one of the leading experts on economics in our time. Yet he had no idea why disaster had struck on his watch, despite the fact that there had been plenty of evidence for decades that should have made him rethink some of his viewpoints.

Lots of complex factors entered into the 2008 recession, including many that went beyond the classic economics that Greenspan knew and espoused (Lewis, 2011; Sorkin, 2009). These factors included aspects of human psychology, a digitized economy, a new casino type of capitalism based on bets and risks with other people's money, a political system largely captured by banks and other large corporations, changes in culture and in ideas about morality, and even the fact that hedge funds were "manned" by testosterone-filled young males eager to outdo one another in the high risks they took (Newton-Small, 2016).

Today there are two new ways to think about intelligence that goes beyond the intelligence of narrow experts left to their own devices. One of these is *wisdom of crowds* or *wisdom of the crowd* (Surowiecki, 2004). The other is *collective intelligence* (Levy, 1999).

In a wisdom of the crowd situation a large number of people—not all of whom, and sometimes none of whom, need be credentialed experts—are asked to offer up their best estimates (guesses) of some quantity or probability, such as election results, sports scores, stock price returns, or even where the next terrorist attack might occur. It turns out that when this is done right, the average (or the majority in some cases) of all responses is more accurate than any given individual response, even a response from an expert.

What does it mean to "do it right"? There are five key things that are necessary for getting a smart crowd. First, the crowd needs to be diverse, so that people can bring different pieces of information to the table. This means that people in the group must come from different backgrounds and have had different experiences in life. Second, the crowd cannot be run top-down. No one person or small group can be determining, manipulating, or influencing the answers. Third, each person in the group must draw on his or her own experiences and backgrounds and not defer to others because of status (by agreeing with them or remaining silent) or for any other reason. Fourth, there must be some incentive or something at stake that motivates people to make their contributions and take the "game" seriously. Fifth, there must be a way to summarize or aggregate people's votes, opinions, answers, or guesses into one collective response.

A good example of the wisdom of crowds in action is seen in the Iowa Electronic Markets (IEM). This is a futures market (a market where people can bet on the future) run by the University of Iowa's Henry B. Tippie College of Business. It is fun for research and teaching purposes. On the IEM people make bets on real-world events such as political outcomes, a company's earnings per share, and stock price returns. People whose bets turn out to be right win a payoff. By and large, when the bets are aggregated (and the conditions for a wise crowd are met), the majority is almost always right and make better predictions than those of experts.

A famous past example of the workings of the wisdom of crowds concerns the *Challenger* disaster (Maloneya & Mulherin, 2003; Surowiecki, 2004). On January 28, 1986, the space shuttle *Challenger* blew up 74 seconds after it launched. Since the launch was televised, the news spread rapidly. Within a very short time the stock market reacted.

Investors quickly dumped their stock in the four large companies—Lockheed, Martin Marietta, Rockwell, and Morton Thiokol—that had been central to the *Challenger* project. However, by the end of the day, Thiokol's stock had taken by far the biggest hit. Investors were clearly trying to figure out who was to blame for the disaster and who would thus have to bear the costs. As these stocks were dropping, no one knew who was to blame. In fact, the morning after the disaster, the *New York Times* concluded there were as yet "no clues to the cause of the accident."

Here, in the words of James Surowiecki, the author of the well-known book *The Wisdom of Crowds* (2004, p. 8), is what this all meant:

> What this means is that the stock market had, almost immediately, labeled Morton Thiokol as the company that was responsible for the Challenger disaster. . . . The steep decline in Thiokol's stock price—especially compared with the slight declines in the stock prices of its competitors—was an unmistakable sign that investors believed that Thiokol was responsible, and that the consequences for its bottom line would be severe.

Though there was as yet no evidence in the media about what company was to blame, the market ending up being right. It was Morton Thiokol. The "crowd" (here, investors) knew something as a crowd that no one individual could be sure of.

COLLECTIVE INTELLIGENCE

The wisdom of crowds phenomenon can be improved upon in ways that carry it over to collective intelligence, referred to above. In the classic wisdom of crowds situation, a large group of people make predictions independently of one another and do not interact with each other. However, if you network the people together, let them share and compare their answers, let them build on each other's answers, and let them discuss things with one another—as well as give them smart tools to use—you can get smart solutions to a wider and more complex array of problems than with the classic wisdom-of-crowds scenario. Furthermore, such groups do not always need to be large.

People networked this way have beaten chess masters at chess; solved scientific problems that have eluded scientists; come up with better designs for things like bikes, shoes, and cars than have official experts; offered innovative solutions to community problems; and much more (Nielsen, 2012). Such collectively intelligent groups operate by the Pareto principle in that 20% of the people make 80% of the suggestions or contributions and 80% make 20% of them. However, remember that everyone can add to or build on or otherwise learn from one another's proposals.

I once listened to a presentation from a man who ran a company that recruited large numbers of people to serve as a collectively intelligent wise crowd to help solve seemingly intractable problems that other businesses paid his company to solve. In the question-and-answer period I asked if the smart crowds he recruited fell into a Pareto distribution where a relatively small number of people made most of the suggestions and the rest made some, but not many, suggestions. He said that they did. I then asked him how often someone in the 80% made a suggestion that turned out to be a crucial part of solving the problem. His answer: "Every time."

COLLECTIVELY INTELLIGENT TEAMS

When people are networked with one another and with smart tools, they can be collectively intelligent even in small groups. We can call these groups *collectively intelligent teams* (Leimeister, 2010). And, indeed, we are all aware that some groups seem to have a collective intelligence that transcends any one person's intelligence in the group. We are also aware that there are groups that seem to have a collective stupidity that transcends any one person's stupidity in the group (in my experience this is often true of committees).

Collective intelligence of all sorts is vitally important in today's world. The world we live in is complex. People and institutions face lots of hard problems that cannot easily be solved with only one set of skills or methods. At the same time, new technologies have greatly enhanced the reach, powers, and possibilities of collective intelligence.

I am concerned here with collectively intelligent teams that share a task. Such teams have the following properties: (1) They connect people with different knowledge and experiences in life but with deep skills for the shared task. These people need not be credentialed experts. (2) Each person in the network is able to understand and coordinate with the skills of the others well enough to meld and integrate his or her own skills with these other people's. They need to be able to do this so that the group can solve problems that cannot be solved by any one person or one set of skills alone. (3) People are networked with one another and with smart tools in ways that give them the resources to share, critically discuss things with each other, and build on each other's work.

A massive multiplayer video game like *World of Warcraft* (*WoW*) is a good example of how collectively intelligent teams operate, though, of course, collective intelligence is also used in much more consequential and important areas. In *WoW* players organize into five-person hunting parties and enter into dungeons to solve problems together. Each person in a party plays a different sort of character with quite different skills and powers in the game. This means that each player has a different specialty (a distinctive skill set), and he or she must be good at it.

At the same time, the game is built so that the problems a hunting party faces cannot be solved with just one or a few different skill sets. So each player in a hunting party not only has to be good at his or her skill set but also must know what the other players can do and how they do it, so the player can use his or her skills in effective concert with those of their other team members.

The players all use pieces of software called "mods" (designed by the company that makes the game or by other players). These mods help players to organize their play; get feedback on their performance; ensure that everyone is pulling their weight; and strategize, individually and as a group, during and after play. For bigger problems (in larger dungeons), several five-person parties can integrate together as modules in a larger group and achieve higher orders of collective intelligence and problem solving.

In business, the *WoW* hunting party is called a "cross-functional team" (Parker, 2002). For example, designers, engineers, manufacturing people, and salespeople may all be on one team. They use smart tools and technologies to network and integrate their skills in order to solve problems that are intractable when everyone stays in their silos and passes on only finished products to others in a linear pipeline. Modern academic research today is often organized as cross-functional teams, defined around hard problems or major challenges, not one discipline alone.

Anita Woolley at Carnegie Mellon and Thomas Malone at MIT (Woolley & Malone, 2011) have found that merely putting smart people in a group does not make the group smart. They found three factors that significantly predicted a group would be smart: (1) the social perceptiveness of the group members, that is, their ability to judge what other people are thinking and feeling, (2) the evenness of conversational turn-taking, with no one person dominating, and (3) the percentage of women in the group.

The last factor is interesting indeed. Woolley and Malone found that more women did not mean just some men and some women. Rather, having some women was better than having none and all-women groups were the best of all. They are not sure why this is so, but it may well be because on average, women score higher on measures of social perceptiveness than do men.

It has been argued more generally that the sorts of social intelligence and networking skills many women tend to have are particularly important in the modern world, where individual "go it alone" expertise can be dangerous (Newton-Small, 2016). Some have even argued, as alluded to above, that the 2008 recession was in part brought on by the testosterone-fueled, high-risk-taking behaviors of young male stockbrokers and hedge fund managers (Coates & Herbert, 2008; Newton-Small, 2016). Things might have been different had there been more women involved or, at least, more collective intelligence drawing on a wider array of skills, perspectives, values, and backgrounds.

ACTIVITY-BASED IDENTITIES

Many activities in the world are organized around a certain "identity." Consider, as an example, a birder (bird-watcher). Certain people are what we might call real birders (Cocker, 2001). By this I mean that they are "into" birding, identify themselves as birders, are adept at birding, and are recognized by other adept birders as a birder.

I should note that there are other sorts of identities than activity-based ones. For example, there are sociocultural identities, as in being an African American of a certain sort; institutional identities, as in being a CEO of a certain sort; socio-nature identities, as in being a male of a certain sort (e.g., a trans male); ideological identities, as in being a radical feminist of a certain sort; ascriptional identities, as in being an A student; and others.

"Real birders" are the people who set the norms and standards for identifying birds in the field and engaging in other aspects of birding (e.g., how to keep a list of the birds you have seen; how to engage in bird counts; what sorts of binoculars and scopes to buy and how to use then; what bird books to use in the field; what to do next when you face a problem in the field; and how to comport yourself when you are in the field with other birders).

In any activity-based identities, there are three types of people. There are "master birders," "adept birders," and "lay birders." Master birders are the top 20% of birders, who do and contribute and know the most. Adept birders are good birders who, nonetheless, do and contribute somewhat less than the masters. The masters are like bishops and the adepts are like priests. Both are what I will call real birders.

Then there are people like me. I love birding as an activity. I respect real birders and I understand and appreciate their judgment system (their values, norms, and ways of engaging in their practices). But I do not consider myself a real birder. This is a choice I have made. If I wanted to—as could anyone—I could commit more and learn, with mentorship, to be a real birder.

I call people like me lay birders. I adopt the term from religion. It is as if the master and adept birders are the higher and lower clergy and the lay birders are the laity who have chosen not to take up a vocation as a priest (let alone a bishop), but see themselves as part of the religion nonetheless. As in a religion, committed laypeople share important understandings about values, meanings, and practices with the clergy.

I have used birding as an example of an activity-based identity. Of course, any society is just chock-full of such identities. Consider, for example, the very partial list below:

Mime
Policeman
Gamer
Kindergarten teacher
Social activist
Linguist
Physicist
Gang member
Doctor
Birder

Fan fiction writer
Craft furniture maker
Carpenter

Some of these are typically jobs, some are not, and some can be jobs for some people and not for others. But I am not concerned with them as jobs, but as ways of being "into" something, of identifying with it. There are certainly master carpenters and biologists and there are adept carpenters and biologists. There are, as well, lay carpenters and biologists. Indeed, today there is a whole DIY biology movement made up of people of all different degrees of expertise, many of whom have no formal biology degrees (Wohlson, 2011). Of course, there are also people who do a job just to earn money and survive, with no real commitment to it as an identity. These people are "doing time." They have a job title, but not an activity-based identity that they own.

Degrees and credentials are secondary here. There are master biologists, historians, and mimes who have no advanced degrees or certifications, and there are people with degrees and certifications who are not really adept at or devoted to what they do. Indeed, today, distributed teaching and learning systems are producing masters, adepts, and laypeople with no degrees or credentials in all sort of areas of interest and passion, including areas of citizen science (Anderson, 2006, 2012; Hatch, 2014; Hitt, 2013; Jenkins, 2006; Shirky, 2008, 2010).

Activity-based identities are another form of collective intelligence, perhaps the most important form in today's world. When someone takes on—as master, adept, or layperson—an activity-based identity, they are networked to the judgment systems, practices, and shared knowledge and skills—as well as the smart tools and other resources— of a large group of people who, through time and space, develop and continually transform effective ways to do certain things and solve certain sorts of problems.

Today there are more activity-based identities than ever before. And new ones are being invented all the time. A great many of these identities are not tied to traditional jobs or institutions but, nonetheless, involve important skills.

Let's take as an example people who play the game *The Sims* and design landscapes, houses, clothes, furniture, and other such things for the game. In the virtual world of *The Sims* players can go to in-game stores to buy (with fictional money) what they need. But they can also use in-game creation tools to design these things themselves.

The tools are user-friendly 3D design tools. Players can go yet further and use 3D design tools and image manipulation tools (e.g., Adobe Photoshop) that are outside the game to make things and input them into the game. People who get good at *Sims* design often give their creations away to other players (the ethical norms of *Sims* designers frowns on selling designs, though one could do so). These activities take place on interest-driven sites devoted to *The Sims* where players share things and information with one another.

Elsewhere I have written about an elderly woman who was unable to go out because of illness but became a widely respected designer of houses, clothes, furniture, and landscapes for *The Sims* (Gee & Hayes, 2010). She eventually gave away more than 14 million designs and had a guest book on her website where over a million people had thanked her and praised her for her designs.

So being a "*Sims* designer" can be an identity if a person identifies with it, understands the judgment system connected to that identity, and can design or appreciate design in the terms that fit the norms and values of the group. Lots of people are lay *Sims* designers in that they engage in the activity and respect the "real designers," know something about their standards, but are into *Sims* design more as a valued hobby than as a vocation.

Activity-based identities are making the modern world go round. They are a large part of what development and schooling ought to be about—though schools confuse "having a job" with "being something" in a world where being something (a committed designer) is more often important than any one job you have.

Every person has different activity-based identities at different levels. For example, I am a master academic in my field, a lay birder, and an adept gamer, and I am an inept, though active, gardener and cook. Academics, birding, and gaming are all important to me and important parts of who I am and of what skills I have.

Like many baby boomer professionals, I spent so much time in life becoming an academic that I did not really develop a lot of other identities at any level (though my academic identity has changed over time). This was not untypical in the "old world," where one could stay something for a long time. This is not a luxury that young people today will have in their future, since jobs will change, old skills will go out of date and new ones will quickly arise, and many people will have to get their sense of competence and belonging "off market" and not from a job title or a large bank account.

Every child today faces a fast-changing, high-risk, and highly complex world. Young people will need to be exposed to a good number of interests and activities and learn to choose wisely which to master, which to become adept at, and which to do as a devoted layperson. They will need to make such choices across a lifetime. The areas where they are masters, adepts, or laypeople will constitute the set of skills and insights that they will need for navigating the future.

SUBJECT MATTER ("CONTENT") IN SCHOOL

What we call a subject matter or content in school is usually a set of facts and information derived from activities that the students are no part of. For example, to biologists biology is not a set of facts but a set of activities (practices) that generate solutions to problems, knowledge, and facts and information. Facts and information serve as tools for solving problems, not as inert matter for memorizing. By the time biology goes to school it becomes textbooks, facts and information, and tests of facts and information, with little or no tie to the activities in which biologists engage, the reasons they do so, and the tools they use.

Even if students have taken a lab, if they do not understand the values, norms, and activities of biologists—do not understand the rules of the games biologists of different types play—then biological facts and information are of little use. They are not retained long, and they do not give rise to any real affiliation with biology (or science in general) as a valued activity, whether or not one wants to become a biologist.

Despite science standards—many of which are quite good—the majority of U.S. students and adults have no deep affiliation with or understanding of science as a "form of life," a way of knowing, doing, and being (Miller & Inglehart, 2012). It is as if we took video games to school and people learned to talk about them but not actually play them and understand what gaming was really all about, as a set of activities to which some people devote themselves with passion.

Outside school, when people become masters, adepts, or laypeople in an area (e.g., *DOTA 2*, media design, carpentry), even the lay people share a good deal of insight into the norms, values, goals, and activities of the area (as these are produced, reproduced, and transformed by the work of the masters and adepts, primarily). Their learning is not inert but based on affiliation and understanding.

Many people today, across the world, engage in citizen science in all sorts of areas (see: science.nasa.gov/citizen-scientists/ and www.citizensciencealliance.org/). Sites or sets of linked sites where people engage in citizen science are often what we have been calling distributed teaching and learning systems. Citizen science has been energized a good deal through the Internet, collaborations between official scientists and citizen scientists, and large databases that citizen scientists can share with official scientists.

A good many citizen scientists are classic laypeople in the domain. They do science to help official scientists and, in the process, they learn a good deal about that science and the judgment system (values, norms, and ways of doing) of that science. Within citizen science of any sort, there are also some people who become master and adept citizen scientists with no official degrees or credentials, but who share a good deal of knowledge and skill with official scientists.

CHAPTER 9

Relational Identities

WHAT WE CAN BE

In the preceding chapter we talked about knowing, doing, and being. We argued that *being* leads to *doing*, because it is people's activity-based identities (whether as a mime, birder, biologist, or carpenter) that give them a judgment system. They use this judgment system to make good choices about how to act and what to do next when things don't work out. Their judgment system also gives them standards and norms, when they act, about what are good results and what are not.

While being leads to effective doing, effective doing leads to dynamic *knowing*. Effective doing, through problem solving, generates facts and information, along with products. In turn, these facts and pieces of information are used as tools for yet more effective *doing* and for transforming the facts and information.

We often ask young people what they want to be when they grow up. By this we usually mean to ask what sort of job they want to have. But today there are many more things to be than those things defined by jobs. There are more things to be today than there have ever been before in history. And there will be ever more new ones in the future. Furthermore, the things to be that matter and count in society are changing radically (Gee, 2013; Jenkins, 2006; Shirky, 2008, 2010).

I pointed out in the preceding chapter that defining what one is (being) in terms of a job is highly problematic today. The vast majority of jobs today are in low-paid service work, and the remainder are manual-labor jobs. Wages, benefits, and union membership have all seriously eroded (Ford, 2015; Reich, 1992, 2010).

Even in the case of white-collar jobs, security is rare. White-collar workers regularly lose their jobs in an economic downturn or when a company changes course. Furthermore, it is common today for companies to shed workers who are 45 and older in favor of younger and cheaper replacements. And it is difficult indeed for these laid-off workers to find equally good jobs or, sometimes, any jobs at all.

We know, too, that a good many types of today's jobs will disappear in the future, and many types of jobs from the recent past have already disappeared. The Internet (as in, e.g., Amazon.com) has been a major job-killer. New types of work will arise, but we cannot predict what kinds of jobs they will be. We also know that we may face a jobless future in which technology and artificial intelligence will lead to far too few jobs for the number of people who need them (Wallach, 2015).

At the same time, the nature of expertise is changing. Thanks to modern technologies and what we called in the previous chapter interest- and passion-driven distributed teaching and learning systems, it is possible today for people of very different ages and backgrounds to become experts in almost any domain without a formal degree or credential. Such people have sometimes been called "Pro-Ams" (professional amateurs; see Anderson, 2006, 2012; Leadbeater & Miller, 2004). Even young people today produce media, games, ads, designs, computer programs, and innovations that are as good as or better than those produced by credentialed experts (Gee, 2013; Hatch, 2014; Hitt, 2013).

Then there are people we might call collective Pro-Ams. These are people who join a group in the real world or on an interest-driven website and learn how to collaborate and pool their skills in order to solve hard problems, make things, or achieve results together that can compete with, and sometimes surpass, credentialed experts, especially those too strongly tied to their narrow silos.

Foldit is a game where everyday people become citizen scientists and see if they can use human pattern recognition to find the optimal folds for proteins, something scientists use supercomputers for. This is important because almost everything that happens in our bodies is the result of proteins. Proteins fold into 3D shapes, rather like origami figures, and there are billions of different shapes they could fold into. However, only one of these is the optimal one that gives rise to the protein's effect. Scientists need to know this shape in order to research and use proteins to cure diseases, for example.

In 2011, a guild in the game *Foldit* discovered the proper fold for the protein that causes AIDS, a feat that had eluded formal scientists for 20 years (Coren & Fast Company, 2011). In the case of collective Pro-Ams, people's expertise is shared with a group and the group's tools and technologies. Their skill is knowing how to use the group's help and resources to lend their skills to collaborative problem solving.

Pro-Ams and collective Pro-Ams (and people can be both) very often do what they do to gain status and a sense of self-worth off-market. They do not do it for money. Sometimes they cannot gain status and worth from their job or their personal identification with their job is low, even if the job pays well. Nonetheless, Pro-Ams often gain skills that can translate into jobs, or they make money from their interests without having a formal institutional job, something that is becoming more and more common (Anderson, 2012; Gee, 2013; Hatch, 2014; Hitt, 2013; Shirky, 2008, 2010).

ACTIVITY-BASED IDENTITIES

Activity-based identities are named by both a noun (for *being*) and a verb (for *doing*). So birders bird, gardeners garden, gamers game, and physicists do physics. However, for any activity-based identity, these general names (e.g., *gardeners, gardening*) hide the large amount of diversity that the activity-based identity encompasses. There are not only many different types of gardeners; there are also many different ways to distinguish between different types of gardeners.

Gardeners can grow one type of plant or many; they can be fruit and vegetable gardeners or flower gardeners or both; they can do organic gardening or not; they can garden to landscape or eat; they can engage in community gardening or garden at home; they can be casual gardeners, high-tech gardeners, large-scale gardeners, or serious gardeners with small plots; they can be container gardeners, raised-bed gardeners, urban gardeners, indoor gardeners, or even butterfly gardeners (growing plants that will attract butterflies). These are only a few of the many different things gardeners can be.

The same thing is true of any other activity-based identity. The true diversity connected to an identity exists in the subtypes (and sub-sub-types, etc.) below the general label.

Activity-based identities are identities that people identify with by free choice. It is important to note, though, that activity-based identities are not *in* a person. They are a reciprocal relationship between a person and a social group and its core defining activities. Such identities change in history as groups change their activities, norms, values, or standards. Some activity-based identities go out of existence and some new ones arise. Activity-based identities are ways for people to identify with something outside themselves, something that other people do and are.

Saint Simeon Stylites (A.D. 390–459) was an ascetic who lived for 37 years on a small platform atop a pillar near Aleppo in Syria. He inspired a 6-century-long succession of *stylitoe*, or pillar hermits (Lent, 2008). Being a pillar hermit is an activity-based identity. Saint Simeon became a saint, but if you tried this today, you would be seen as mentally ill. The niche for pillar hermits is now long gone. Of course, it might come back, though I doubt it. But for now, it is gone and you're out of luck if you want to be one. For Saint Simeon to be a pillar hermit, people had to recognize and accept that he was one (and understand what it meant) and others had to become one, too.

Activity-based identities are like a marriage freely chosen. They are, we might say, marriages for love. However, there are a large number of other sorts of identities that are much more like arranged marriages. Sometimes people in arranged marriages end up in love, sometimes they don't, but it is not all that easy to leave the marriage in many cases. The myriad of different activity-based identities and their diverse internal subtypes are not usually what educators and policymakers mean when they talk about diversity. They more often mean these other sorts of identities that are much more like arranged marriages. These are what I will call *relational identities.*

RELATIONAL IDENTITIES

Relational identities are defined in terms of relations, contrasts, or oppositions between different types of people. Here is a nonexhaustive list:

Identities	Examples
Cultural	Native American, Latino
Ascribed	ADHD, gifted
Gender	woman, trans man
Sexuality	heterosexual, gay
Attributes	cancer survivor, deaf
Ideological	conservative, libertarian
Religious	Christian, Hindu
Class	working class, 1%
Family	the Smith family, the Billings lineage
Age	teen, elderly

Relational identities are often imposed on or assigned to people, the result of "fate," or picked up in early socialization in life within families. Even political viewpoints like being liberal or conservative are strongly connected to our families and upbringing.

Each of these sorts of relational identities can exist in three separate ways: (1) a classificatory label that other people apply to you but that you reject or don't much care about, (2) a label that you own and identify with, and (3) a label you are conflicted about.

As classifications, relational identities can be problematic in a number of ways. First, unlike activity-based identities, such as gamer or gardener, these identities are relational. They are defined in relation to, and often in contrast or opposition to, other identities. Teens are defined in relation and contrast to other age groups. Native Americans are defined in relation and contrast to other ethnic groups. People with ADHD are defined in relation and contrast to other people with disabilities and abilities. When humans start classifying by oppositions and contrasts, distinctions all too often become invidious, caught up with "better" and "worse" sorts of judgments.

Relational identities change or disappear if the other identities they are contrasted with change or disappear. If humans died by the age of 20 or so, there would be no need for a *teen* category (teens then would just be adults) and the category of *elderly* would change quite a bit. If all non–African American people in the United States disappeared tomorrow, then African Americans would cease to be African Americans and would become just Americans. Conservatives in the United States have moved so far to the right over the past few decades that politicians once seen as conservative would now be viewed as moderates (e.g., President Dwight Eisenhower).

Such relational identities can easily get caught up with invidious comparisons and hierarchies, as I pointed out above. First, for example, why do we regularly and obsessively refer to some American Black people as African American because some of them had an ancestor hundreds of years ago in Africa, but next to no one ever refers to me as a British American because I had ancestors in England long ago?

African Americans are "special" in the sense of being singled out as eternally hyphenated while a great many other groups have lost their hyphens (or have them merely as honorifics). Indeed, it is hard to think of any group more indigenously American, aside from Native Americans, than African Americans. After all, they have been in America longer and contributed more to the country than almost any other Americans, but they keep their hyphen, nonetheless.

Second, though relational identities are the categories that define what *diversity* means to educators, they can actually efface diversity. Relational identities are at such a high level of generality that they can efface the myriad real differences between Latinos, Christians, elderly people, and so on for all the other categories. In all these categories, the differences between people in them swamp any commonalities they have as a big group. There is tremendous diversity among African Americans (not to mention "Blacks," a much wider group), Latinos, and the elderly. Why? Because all of them have lived out lives defined by many more attributes than being African American, Latino, or elderly.

These big relational categories are at the wrong level to define real diversity. Diversity exists at the next level down. Just as the diversity in gardening exists in the many different types of gardeners and even the many different ways to identify such types, diversity in regard to relational identities exists at the level of different types of African Americans, elderly people, working-class people, and conservatives. It exists at the level at which individual people in these categories have distinctive experiences that, though connected to the larger category, differ based on their own unique selves and distinctive positions in life and trajectories across time and space.

Third, relational identities can efface individuality. People are the products of their unique genetic and epigenetic makeup and experiences in life. Each person's unique tapestry is too often effaced by the way many people use relational identity labels, which tend to be totalizing. There are times for everyone when a nonrelational activity-based identity trumps one of these relational labels. Sometimes a good gamer or fan fiction writer wants to be a "real" gamer or fan fiction writer and not "just" an African American or Latino or Anglo-American gamer or fan fiction writer.

Individuality is genetic, epigenetic, physical, environmental, social, and cultural. It is the product of interactions between a person's body/brain, environment, and social interactions. But the dynamics of these interactions happen closer to the ground of lived reality and diverse experiences than these more general relational identity categories allow for.

Fourth, relational identities are often used and abused in ways that efface history. Each one of these categories has had a long history of having been invented, produced and reproduced, and transformed across time and in terms of a great many vested interests. There is nothing "natural" about any these categories, though we often treat them as if there were.

Take the category "Asperger's disease" as an example (Baron-Cohen & Klin, 2006). For most of history no such category existed. In 1944 it came into existence, thanks to the Austrian pediatrician Hans Asperger (1906–1980). However, in 2013, the DSM-5 replaced Autistic Disorder, Asperger's Disorder, and other, related developmental disorders with the umbrella term "autism spectrum disorder" (American Psychiatric Association, 2013). Asperger's disease disappeared. It may come back, or it may not.

When I was growing up in San Jose, California, in the 1950s, some Italian American friends of ours bought a new house in a better neighborhood than their old one. People in the new neighborhood picketed with signs that said, "No Blacks." Today many Italian Americans have long lost their double descriptors (except for holidays), and no one can seem to remember when they were "Black."

My own heritage is in a group of people who have been called things like White trash, hillbillies, trailer trash, and more. This group of people has existed since long before the founding of the United States (Isenberg, 2016). Indeed, related terms of abuse were already common in England before any English person set foot in America, and the epithets were retained when they did. These terms included *lubbers, rubbish, clay eaters*, and *crackers*. One interesting term that the English at home and in the American colonies used for such people was *offscourings*, which meant "human fecal waste."

Historically the term *trash* in *White trash* is related to waste and a peculiarly British view of waste. In precolonial and colonial times, the word *waste* was applied to both people and land. Land was *wasteland* if no one cultivated it or made it otherwise commercially productive. *Waste people* owned no land and drifted from place to place. They were unproductive people and, thus, they were "waste," like unproductive land.

This group, whatever we call it, has played a significant role in U.S. history—though in different subgroups, known as, for example, Southern White trash, hillbillies, or Western squatters. It has been repeatedly used as a model of degenerate culture and has often been juxtaposed, in complex ways, with African American people as a way to ensure that poor Whites and Blacks did not (and do not now) join in common cause. Indeed, this group—my people—may be the only one left that has no label that isn't derogatory. History matters, not least for those who are products of it.

Fifth, activity-based identities exist because a person identifies with the activity and the people who do it. If they did not so identify, they would not join the activity. But relational identities are imposed on people, whether or not they identify with the identity themselves. People can be trapped in them as stereotypes largely defined by others if they do not choose to identify with them themselves.

RELATIONAL IDENTITIES AS OWNED, REJECTED, OR CONFLICTED

Relational identities as labels stem from the work that institutions and social groups have done through history to classify people (Hacking, 1985, 1994). In turn, these classifications come to define how we treat people in the category, though in reality the people in the category are quite diverse and, thus, one size never fits all here.

However, people can choose to own and identify with a relational identity. For them, then, it is not just a classification that was imposed on them or that they inherited. It is how they see themselves. For example, some deaf people see deafness not just as a socially significant attribute but also as a valuable and distinctive culture with its own language (ASL) and ways of being, doing, and knowing. They refer to themselves as Deaf, with a capital *D*, and in this way turn a classification (deaf) into an identity they highly value and accept (Padden & Humphries, 2005). Being big-*D* Deaf is defined not by how much hearing you do or do not have, but by values, norms, and activities in which people engage together.

A relational identity can thus become much like an activity-based identity. Being big-*D* Deaf is an example. Here is another: I was raised a devout Catholic. Since I was baptized as a baby, I clearly did not choose this religion. It was imposed on me. But I strongly identified with its activities, things like going to Mass, being an altar boy, teaching catechism, going to confession, attending retreats, and many more. I was a "real Catholic" in the way in which someone can be a real mime or a real gamer, as described earlier.

Some other Catholics identified in no deep way with Catholic activities. They came to church irregularly and saw Catholicism as an inherited culture. We called such people "Catholics in name only," though we accepted them still, in some sense and for some occasions, as fellow Catholics.

There were also people who identified with Catholic activities, but did not accept all the church's beliefs, though they did not make this public. They wanted a religion for their own lives and for what they conceived of as the good of their children. They were active in the church and committed to its activities. I did not then have a name for such people, since I did not know they existed until I left the church. When people left the church, by the way, we called them "lapsed Catholics." It was hard to get away from the label. At the most general level Catholics define someone as forever Catholic if they were baptized as a Catholic.

People can even freely identify with relational identities like bipolar disorder sufferer or cancer survivor (Martin, 2007). They see such an identity not just as a label someone else has given them but as a way of being in the world connected to special ways of doing and knowing. They sometimes even join with others to celebrate the identity and redefine it in positive terms. This is one way they seek to own the identity rather than be trapped in it.

If a person does not personally identify with a relational identity, then I will simply say they fall into a relational classification that some other people have made up for them. The trouble is that for people who do not want to identify with these relational identities, it can be very hard to opt out.

Too often in education, what passes for a discussion about diversity is really a conversation about these relational identities as classifications. What passes for multiculturalism can sometimes be more a celebration of classifications than of actually lived and shared experiences of people who almost always, in reality, make up many smaller subkinds of the kind of people being defined by the classificatory label.

If we really wanted to celebrate diversity at school we would celebrate the identities that people actively identify with and ask how they identify with them, which is different for different people who share the same label. We should never assume Juan or Janie is an X unless we come to know how they identify with X, if they do at all.

Diversity should also mean the very complex ways in which people relate to these categories. There are many nuances in identifying with a label (though always in certain specific ways, not in general) and not identifying with it.

For example, as I said above, my background is in people who have been referred to as White trash, waste people, and hillbillies, among many other labels, since well before the founding of the United States. I have a very complex and conflicted relationship with this category and the big and diverse group of people it indiscriminately labels. The relationship is far too complex to say either that I identify or don't identify with this group. It is a matter of love, loyalty, fear, loathing, and pity. That's my story, and if you wanted to honor my "diversity" you would have to listen to it, not generalize on the basis of what is, in reality, a rough-and-ready and "other infected" (not self-defined) category.

Now, of course, it is possible I should be less conflicted about my heritage. Possibly I have been duped into these conflicts by other people's opinions (people who, by and large, really know nothing about my group). And, admittedly, when I began to read the history of so-called White trash, I learned new ways to think about these people and myself and, also, America. In fact, one of the most important things education could do for people is let them know the complex history of interactions and relationships between and within relational identities.

I am not, by any means, saying that these relational identity categories are not important. Indeed, they make up the social geography of society (Gee, 1990/2015b, 2015a). They are the level at which many people are advantaged or disadvantaged, thanks to other people with other labels. What I am saying is that they are not the level at which diversity of the sort that gives rise to collective intelligence exists. That level is made up of living, breathing, multifaceted people with a great many varieties of experiences and identities who may happen to be labeled X and may or may not identify with X or may have an entirely complex relationship with X. That they are X is important (because it affords and constrains the experiences they have); how they are X is even more important.

I have acknowledged that people can, and often do, turn a relational identity not just into an owned identity but also into a cherished one indeed. In many cases, such cherishing has been a crucial survival device for people and a prime motivation for demands for respect and fairness. But, alas, such cherishing sometimes—too often—comes at the cost of disdaining people with other labels.

DEVELOPMENT

What develops is a person, not a category. In my view, the best way to look at relational identities is as social constructs that have the power both to make certain sorts of experiences readily available and to constrain or block certain sorts of experiences people can have in the world. My devout Catholic upbringing gave me the experience of things like meditation, social work, and confession. It also heavily constrained my experiences with girls and women, with media, and with people in other religions.

It is important, for any relational identity, to ask what special and life-enhancing experiences a person has been afforded by this identity. Since it is a complex person who has the experience, not a category, we must also ask how these experiences were brought to life differently by different people with the same relational identity.

It is also important to ask, for any relational identity, what constraints on experience a person may have faced. In turn, we need to help all people gain new experiences under new or newly chosen and owned identities, not the least of which are activity-based identities.

Almost all relational identities—whether being rich, being poor, having ADHD, or being a Catholic—have brought people with that identity both important and insightful experiences others have not had, and also brought them constraints and limitations on experience, constraints and limitations that others have not had. Fortunately, most people (but, alas, not all) can choose new identities to make up for limitations on old ones (without having to give up the old ones, if they don't want to). And they can bring the special experiences their relational identities have afforded them as "capital" for collective intelligence and human progress.

Educators often celebrate and even romanticize "culture," especially that of some oppressed peoples (not all). But all cultures have good and bad elements. Culture is a source of social nourishment and survival. It is also the source of othering people and sometimes of exclusion and conflict.

Humans are frail beings and the cultures they create are marvels, but vexed ones. While we most certainly should celebrate multiculturalism, we should also celebrate the lived mess of complexity that is true diversity. Because, in the end, it is only lived, owned, and experientially grounded diversity that fuels the collective intelligence and collaboration that can save us poor humans and the rest of the living world we have so imperiled.

CHAPTER 10

Affinity Space

BECOMING A GAMER: DEVELOPMENT

In 2002, when I was 53 years old, I played my first video game (Gee, 2007). I had a 6-year-old son who had enjoyed interactive digital books on the computer since he was 2, books such as *Winnie-the-Pooh* and those by Dr. Seuss. These interactive books eventually led me to buy him a video game called *Pajama Sam: No Need to Hide When It's Dark Outside*.

In the game, Sam, a little boy, is tired of being afraid of the dark. To face his fear, he transforms himself into Pajama Sam, the world's youngest superhero, and goes out to find Darkness in his closet. Inside the closet, he enters a world where, with the help of King (a mine car) and Otto (a boat), he eventually confronts and befriends Darkness. The game involves solving puzzles and thinking strategically to help Sam on his journey.

I knew that interacting around books with your child was good for literacy development, so I figured I would sit with Sam and interact with him around the game as a newer type of media. It was a fascinating experience. The game was fun and the problem solving was interesting. The game allowed a 6-year-old child and an older adult to problem-solve together. There were aspects of the game at which he was better and others where I was better. It was a real collaboration.

As we played *Pajama Sam* I wondered what an adult video game would be like. So I went out and bought one. Of course, I had no idea what to get. I chose what turned out to be a not very well-known game called *The New Adventures of the Time Machine*. I probably got the game because of the title's illusion to H. G. Wells's *The Time Machine*.

I found the game hard, long, and frustrating. I was amazed that people paid for this sort of experience. I failed and failed again. For the first time in years, I was learning something completely new, no longer able just to rest on the laurels of my past experiences, nearly all of which were irrelevant to this new one.

I confronted myself as a new learner—and not just a well-practiced expert—for the first time in decades and was not pleased with what I found. The experience forced me to persist past failure a great many times. It eventually forced me to take risks and try new things after I had perseverated in the same bad strategy over and over again to no good effect. Indeed, my 6-year-old, seeing me fail again and again at a problem in the game, said to me, "Why don't you try something different this time?" (Now, there's a good learning principle!)

I eventually found playing the game life-enhancing. The combination of difficulty and frustration, on the one hand, and new growth and development, on the other, was painful and joyous at the same time. Furthermore, I eventually discovered that my experience playing this game, and later ones, illuminated issues about literacy and learning I had long studied. This was a surprise and, at the same time, an opportunity that I would not have had, had I never picked up *The New Adventures of the Time Machine*.

By the time I played my second game—it took me a long time to finish the first one—I had discovered game sites and gamers and picked one of the greatest games of all time, the first *Deus Ex*. I had begun having access to the judgment system of real gamers. It would, of course, be a long haul before I internalized and was able to use—and even later yet contribute to—that judgment system.

Video games like *Deus Ex*, *Half-Life*, *System Shock 2*, and *Castlevania: Symphony of the Night* (my subsequent games) are long and hard and require persistence. They are not always fun, they can be hard and frustrating, but they are always engaging. Though I could never have predicted it, when, after years of play, I had become a "real gamer," I came to know people like Warren Specter, the well-known game designer who was the lead designer on *Deus Ex*.

I began with *Pajama Sam*. I ended as a gamer. In between these two points is development, which, if I continue to seek out new challenges in gaming and don't rest on my past laurels, will continue. What I am concerned with here is how to understand such development.

I have played a great many games for thousands of hours. I have written books, journal articles, and magazine pieces on games. I have given many talks across the world on games, not just at academic conferences but also at the annual Game Developers Conference (GDC) and at E3 (the industry's trade show) and other places where gamers and game designers gather.

I have done consulting for game companies, and I helped two young people start one that specializes in games for learning. I helped start a program and conference on games, society, and culture at the University of Wisconsin–Madison. I have given a great many interviews on games to TV, radio, Internet, and print media. I have blogged about games, both on my own site and for other Internet sites.

I have served on the advisory boards or boards of directors for game projects and start-ups. I now know a great many people who are into gaming, including gamers at all different levels, game designers, game journalists, and game academics. I keep up with lots of game sites and gamer news. I even once played a very difficult game—the first *Ninja Gaiden*—in front of 1,500 people while giving a formal lecture about games, game design, and learning. And I didn't die once.

DEVELOPMENT AS A JOURNEY THROUGH SPACES

So, I am "into" games. I am a "real gamer," though not a top one. The journey from *Pajama Sam* to where I am now (and where I hope to go) is how I want to think about development: as a journey. Since schools stress knowing (really retention and recall), not being and doing, we tend to think of development as an internal journey taken in the mind. Researchers focus on changes in cognitive mental processing.

But there is another way to think about development when what is developing is *being* that leads to *doing* that, in turn, leads to *knowing*. My development from *Pajama Sam* to an "into it" gamer was a journey through different *spaces* (real and virtual) across time, spaces filled with different sorts of people, technologies, media, resources, and tools relevant to gaming and becoming a gamer.

My journey through these spaces was unique. It was unique not because of anything about me, but because all such journeys—all paths of development—are unique. There are different routes to becoming something. And different people, based on who they are and what else they have experienced in life, take different routes and end up in somewhat different places on the gamer map.

As I said earlier, real diversity is not at the level of general labels, like *gamer*, *physicist*, or *Catholic*. Diversity exists at the next level down in terms of different subtypes (and sub-subtypes) of gamers, physicists, and Catholics. These subtypes rarely have names. They are based on different rites of passage across a shared land, but a land with many different paths to be carved out.

Here are just some of the spaces I moved through early in my journey. Not atypically, many spaces I ended up in were matters of luck and good fortune, not real planning. In each space, I was mentored and taught.

My first step was reading interactive books with my 6-year-old at home. The next step was buying *Pajama Sam* at a game store. After that I took the step of buying *The New Adventures of the Time Machine* and later *Deus Ex*. I came to know more about how to use video game stores (and their clerks) and game sites as key resources. As I played more and more, I wanted to write about games because I saw connections between gaming and my work on learning and literacy. So I continued to play; learn about games, gamers, and gaming; and write.

When I was finishing up my first book on games, Henry Jenkins, one of the world's leading media scholars and then at MIT, got wind of the book I was writing and called me out of the blue. He introduced himself and told me that he was surprised someone that he did not already know was writing about games. Through Henry, I ended up meeting the first generation of young gamer academics (people like Kurt Squire), getting involved with some game and media conferences, and giving my first interview on games (with Henry for PBS).

The famed tech magazine *Wired* also heard about the book in progress and asked me to write a very short piece about the book for their magazine. They found my writing too academic (surprise, surprise) and rewrote the piece for me. Very few of my words were left (thank God). This piece has been reprinted, as a model of good persuasive writing, several times in books on writing. As a literacy scholar, I knew authorship was social; I just didn't know it was *this* social.

The people who organize the annual Game Developers Conference (GDC—a very big deal in the game world) saw the *Wired* piece and asked me to give a talk at GDC (I was one of the first academics to be so invited). I talked about gaming to an audience partly composed of people who had designed some of the games I had written about in my book. Several of these people eventually became friends and colleagues.

Through GDC I met other people and made contact with other organizations—and found out about all sorts of gamer sites, game media, and gamer resources—that led to other spaces and other people at other times. The journey was begun and took a winding path through a great many unpredictable spaces, in each of which I was mentored and taught.

There was no one space (like a classroom), but many. There was no one teacher, but many. There was no textbook. Things developed in my head, in terms of *cognition* and *feeling*, as well as *valuing*. But things also developed in my fingers, eyes, and body, as I became a better gamer and a better participant in, and observer of, gaming as a set of different, but related, activities.

Things also got developed, not just in me, but by me (with many others) in the world, things such as new sorts of games, new game companies, new game research, and new game conferences. Eventually, I myself became parts of spaces where people could come to get mentored and taught on their journey.

Other people's journeys to being a gamer were not the same as mine. There are lots and lots of different types of gamers. But we diverse gamers are, nonetheless, all "fellow travelers," who (often, but not always, of course) help one another on the way, even if it is only to wave as we cross paths, though it is often to invite one another in or to point one another in a new direction. That is how I want to look at development.

Unfortunately, as we know from controversies like Gamergate, some gamers have displayed demeaning sexism toward women in gaming. As is so often the case in media, the bad apples were taken as the whole orchard. There are bad people everyone, and good ones too, and sometimes they are the same people at different times and in different contexts. I, as an old academic gamer, have been dismissed by some hard-core "fanboys" (a term of art). But I have experienced immensely more acceptance and camaraderie from gamers of all ages, skill levels, and genders than I have rejection.

At the ever-widening edge of gaming today, where most of the true innovation occurs, there are many superbly intelligent and highly creative women, among them Mary Flanagan, Tracy Fullerton, Robin Hunicke, Katherine Isbister, Colleen Macklin, Katie Salen, Constance Steinkuehler (just to name a few I know personally), and many others. It is crucial in creative endeavors to realize that growth and innovation occur at the margins and not at the dead center, despite the fact that the center gets most of the attention until the innovations themselves become mainstream. This is true too, in my view, of most academic areas. There are, of course, women who are today—and some who have long been—at the center in gaming (many lists are available on the Internet)—and I love standard AAA games—but my interests have always been at the spots where innovation is seeping up out of the ground [End of Editorial].

I am using my development as a gamer as just one example. Though it might seem special, I want to suggest that it is typical. Such journeys through different spaces are the norm when someone journeys to *being* a real gamer, gardener, physicist, Catholic, or African American.

I know it may seem odd to talk about real Catholics or real African Americans. After all, aren't all Catholics and all African-Americans real? Yes, they are (if they want to be). Nonetheless, some Catholics or African Americans are really into these identities. They seek out experiences and mentorship to gain standards (a judgment system) about what should count as one type (not all types) of being an into-it Catholic or African American.

WHY AFFINITY SPACE?

One thing is misleading about my description of my development as a gamer as a journey. I have made the journey sound like a linear movement from one place to another, like a one-way trip from San Jose, California, to Amherst, Massachusetts. But development is a journey that continually moves back and forth between new and old spaces. It revisits many of the same spaces, stays in some a long while, in others a short time. The spaces evolve over time, in part because of who visits them and what they do there. Furthermore, the journey need not have any final destination. People can keep seeking new challenges, keep learning new things, and thus keep developing.

So I need a name for the spaces through which people with a shared interest or passion can move back and forth to develop into and be a certain kind of person, such as a gamer, a Catholic, or a physicist. I will call such spaces *affinity spaces* (Gee, 2004, 2007, 2015a; Gee & Hayes, 2010, 2011).

Spaces like the annual GDC, E3 (the game industry's major trade show), LAN parties (where people network their computers together in one place to play games together), multiplayer game play from home with others around the world via the Internet, gaming shows on Twitch TV, and game sites of all sorts are affinity spaces in the gaming world. I call them affinity spaces because such spaces invite an affiliation with gamers and gaming and people can come to them to experience a shared interest in gaming (at the level of either interest or passion).

Even my game room at home is a gamer affinity space. When people visit my game room, they enter a gamer space. Not many people come, but if someone new comes he or she will see and feel an affinity for gaming and gamers and have access to sharing in or learning about that affinity.

Now, talking about space has a naming problem. Spaces are like places (the only difference is that I am using the word *space* to include both physical places and virtual ones). Places can be inside one another like nested boxes: My farm is in Cottonwood, Cottonwood is in northern Arizona, northern Arizona is in the state of Arizona, Arizona is in the western United States, the western states are in the United States of America, the United States is in the continent of North America, and so on, till we get to the world as a whole and even the universe.

Places can also be connected to each other without one place being inside the other. So Arizona is near Mexico, New Mexico, Nevada, and Colorado, but none of these places are inside any of the others and one is in a different country altogether.

The same two things are true of affinity space. *The Sims* gamer affinity space is part of the larger gamer/gaming affinity space. In turn, it is composed of many smaller spaces such as forums devoted to *The Sims*, *The Sims* interest-driven websites of all different sorts, *The Sims* conferences, and many others. These are all parts of the larger *Sims* affinity space, and some of them have smaller subspaces within them.

There can be connections between spaces in different affinity spaces; for example, many people are both into playing *The Sims* and into writing graphic fan fiction connected to *The Sims*. This is to say that some people move back and forth between some spaces in *The Sims* gamer affinity space and some spaces in *The Sims* fan fiction affinity space. Both of these can be seen as (large) parts of *The Sims* affinity space (devoted to anything to do with *The Sims*).

So, like physical space, affinity spaces are nested inside one another, are connected to one another, and exist at different levels from small to large. They can be mapped out and their parts can be named. They are the multiple spaces that allow for the looping journeys that constitute and sustain development. Affinity spaces constitute the geography of development.

The difference between affinity spaces like gamer affinity space or Catholic affinity space and the places that make up the United States is that in an affinity space people share an affinity for (an interest in or a passion for) some shared identity connected to some shared activities, values, and norms. Perhaps this was once true of the United States (in which case the United States would have been an affinity space in which people journeyed to become "real Americans"), but if it ever was, it seems so no longer. It is an interesting question whether there is any level—from neighborhoods through towns and cities and states to regions—at which Americans share enough with one another to constitute an affinity space.

What I am calling affinity spaces are not new, but digital media are radically transforming them (Jenkins, 2006). To understand these transformations, it is best to start with traditional affinity space. Here, rather than gaming, I will use being a Catholic at the time of my youth as my example.

CATHOLIC AFFINITY SPACE

When I was young (long ago), I was part of a very devout Catholic family that interacted almost exclusively with fellow Catholics. What I will call a *Catholic affinity space* was a big part of our lives. This Catholic affinity space was made up of smaller affinity spaces and routes between them. These smaller affinity spaces (all located in the larger Catholic affinity space) included our home (with its religious statues and images, places for devotional activities, and a room filled with religious books); other people's Catholic homes; our elementary school; our parish church; the local Catholic high school and college, where it was assumed we would all end up once we left elementary school; other local Catholic churches where we attended baptisms, confirmations, weddings, and funerals of Catholic friends in other parishes; Catholic churches we attended when on vacation; sites where adults or families attended religious events outside the school or church, such as retreats or gatherings to hear speakers; sites where the school or church carried out social events such as dinners or charity events; and the cathedral for the diocese, a place we went to rarely, but which was a looming presence nonetheless. There were many more relevant spaces as well. Figure 10.1 sketches out but a small section of (just a few of the locations in) this affinity space.

I call this set of affinity spaces a part of a larger Catholic affinity space (there are many more spaces in it) because people were connected to one another in it (as they moved across different affinity spaces within the larger Catholic affinity space) by their shared affinity for Catholicism. I will call Catholicism (as a set of ideas, values, and activities) the *attractor* to the Catholic affinity space. The attractor is

Figure 10.1. Some of the Spaces in the Catholic Affinity Space

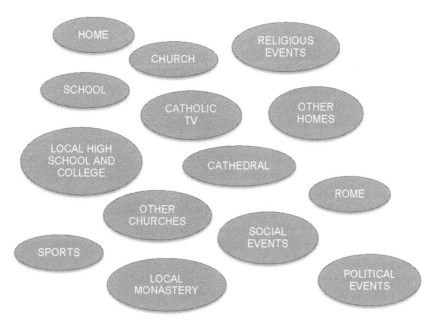

the thing for which people who move around in the big space have a shared interest or passion. It also beckons to anyone who enters any part of the space and seeks to entice him or her to stay in the space.

Everyone who entered any part of the Catholic affinity space because of an interest in or passion for Catholicism I will call an *affine*. By this I mean that such people, even if they were just "looking," were potential allies and recruits for Catholic development.

Clumps of people who overlapped a good deal in various subspaces (locations) of the larger Catholic affinity space and thus bumped into one another rather regularly, I will call *fellow travelers*. The notion of "fellow travelers" is "squishy," that is, not well-bounded, since there is no definitive amount of overlap that determines "membership" and since people can drop in and drop out as time passes.

Some of the spaces in the larger Catholic affinity space were special. They were what I will call *home bases*. Home bases are key places where fellow travelers come together a good deal to engage in the activities that keep their shared affinity alive. They are places where the people with the most passion for the shared affinity are the key organizers, motivators, teachers, and standard-setters for the affinity space as a whole. For us, there were three home bases: home, school, and the parish church.

These three home bases were closely connected. Priests, nuns, and other families regularly visited our home; we regularly visited other homes, our church, and our school. Priests from the church visited the school for religious instruction and the nuns from the school regularly ran events at the church for their students and their families. We might call home-school-church here a *home-base cluster*.

Finally, let us note that some of the subspaces in the Catholic affinity space were used for other purposes and were, thus, subparts of other affinity spaces as well. For example, our parish church was linked to a variety of other spaces—some not specifically Catholic—that constituted an affinity space to combat Communism (this was the 1950s, after all). This anti-Communist affinity space overlapped with our Catholic affinity space (e.g., we took an anti-Communist course in elementary school whose textbook was titled *The Evil Tree*), but it was, by and large, more central for some families than for others. Nonetheless, because of this overlap, I was (even as a child) an affine of the people in this anti-Communist affinity space.

The Catholic affinity space I have sketched out here was made up primarily of physical spaces and physical routes. But not all of them were physical. There was no Internet then, but telephones served as routes to connect spaces within the larger affinity space. Further, a great many of us "religiously" watched Bishop Fulton J. Sheen's *Life Is Worth Living* television show each week (1951–1957) and later the *Fulton Sheen Program* (1961–1968). Such televised spaces were much like, though less interactive than, digital virtual worlds. So the Catholic affinity space was composed of physical spaces and routes and less physical sorts of spaces and routes.

Each affinity space in the larger overall affinity space in Figure 10.1 was a site where learning, mentoring, or teaching could go on, differently for different sorts of people (e.g., young people, converts, returning Catholics, devout Catholics seeking to deepen their faith). It is important to note that learning, mentoring, and teaching in a larger affinity space like the Catholic affinity space is distributed across different spaces, people, and practices. Teaching and learning about Catholicism by no means took place in only our Catholic school; it occurred in almost all the spaces within the large Catholic affinity space as a whole.

The school was not isolated from the other spaces in the larger affinity space. Indeed, it was "porous" to these other spaces. People, ideas, artifacts, and practices circulated among different spaces, including the school.

Every subspace was related to every other in the larger Catholic affinity space by shared affinity for Catholicism. Every space shared in the responsibility for teaching, mentoring, and resourcing Catholic development at all different levels. Since teaching and learning were distributed across different spaces, people, and activities, this Catholic affinity space was also a prime example of what I earlier called a distributed teaching and learning system.

SCHOOLS AS ISOLATED

In a pluralistic and ideologically divided society like the United States (and a great many other countries), public schools tend to become isolated from other spaces. The people in them often share few interests, passions, values, and norms that could guide them together in looping journeys between multiple affinity spaces within a larger shared affinity space that composed them all. The school becomes the main and only site for teaching and learning academic skills. Teaching and learning are, thus, not well distributed.

Public schools do often have partial alliances with certain sorts of families who prepare their children for school at home and support their schooling thereafter. This is, of course, a bit of distribution of teaching and learning. However, many families form no such alliances, at least at any deep level. Some families do not have the time, resources, or knowledge needed to form such an alliance. Some do not share enough values with the school to form an alliance with it, sometimes to such a degree that they avoid the public schools altogether. And, too, there is often much less passion for learning and development in school than there is in any affinity space at any level. After all, it is hard to beat avoiding an eternity of suffering in hell as a motivator.

We will see in the next chapter that the power that affinity spaces like Catholicism had for distributing teaching and learning in service of developing passion is now becoming common on the Internet for a great many different activities that can underwrite different identities. So what can schools do? How can they compete with passion?

How can they ensure that all children, not just ones with proactive mentors at home, have the opportunity to take some new interests all the way to the sorts of passion that fuel deep identification and deep skill development? Can schools become introducers to, curators of, aggregators of, mentors for, and sometimes even joint subspaces within diverse and valuable affinity spaces? (This question and suggestion comes from Jeff Holmes, my former graduate student, who has written eloquently about distributed teaching and learning systems; see Holmes, 2016.)

CHAPTER 11

New Affinity Spaces

AFFINITY SPACES IN A DIGITAL WORLD

As we saw in the preceding chapter, affinity spaces existed in the past, long before digital media. What is new today is that there are a great many more affinity spaces and they have a lot more virtual spaces in them.

Affinity spaces are becoming the prime places where people engage in 21st-century teaching, learning, doing, and being. As a result, we have to begin thinking of space as a physical and virtual meld.

Affinity spaces are primarily defined by an affinity for solving certain sorts of problems. As such, they always involve the development of specific sorts of skills. My Catholic affinity space dealt with the problems that most religions deal with: problems about how and why to act morally, why bad things happen to good people, and the meaning of life. Catholic theology introduced me to interpretative, hermeneutic, historical, philosophical, and linguistic (e.g., Latin) ideas and skills that have transferred to my later academic work.

Today you probably could not name a problem that is not an attractor to one or more affinity spaces. Such problems include media production, citizen science, political activism, women's health, fan fiction writing, video games, specific diseases, and almost anything else you can name. In these affinity spaces people act, teach, learn, and produce without regard to credentials, age, outside status, or degrees of expertise.

VIDEO GAMES AND AFFINITY SPACE

Now I want to discuss one specific area—video games—where we can see potential uses of affinity spaces for teaching and learning. Video games have become an area where we, as educators, have something

117

to learn about how to organize interest and passion (Gee, 2004, 2007, 2015a). This is not a plea to use video games in school. It is a plea to use video games for thinking about and reflecting on how to improve teaching and learning, with or without games.

A video game is just a set of well-designed problems to solve. The design of the game teaches and mentors players to solve the problems, using good principles of teaching and learning. A game can be designed around any well-defined and challenging set of problems, for example, designing civilizations (*Civilization*), fighting wars (*Call of Duty*), solving algebra equations (*Dragon Box*), building a family and community (*The Sims*), or cleaning a house when you are a four-inch-tall house-cleaning robot (*Chibi-Robo*).

Gamers do not just play games. When they have a real interest or passion for a game or a type of game, they often take their game-based learning into modern affinity spaces.

For many gamers, their gaming room at home is connected not only to the virtual spaces of the games themselves but also to other interest-driven Internet sites where they discuss, learn about, and teach about the games they play. For these gamers, their gaming rooms are also connected to other physical spaces, such as gaming rooms in friends' homes; LAN parties; stores where gamers gather; gamer conventions; gamer clubs; and, perhaps, too, places where they play nondigital tabletop games.

This whole set of physical and virtual spaces that characterize the comings and goings of gamers is an affinity space composed of many other subspaces. These sorts of affinity spaces today are often "squishy." They are fluid and ever-changing. They are hard to strictly demarcate. Spaces and subspaces come, go, and transform as the interest/passion that fuels them evolves and as technologies change.

Each gamer takes different looping itineraries through gamer affinity space. We could, if we liked, map out for each person, at any period of time, what parts of the affinity space he or she inhabits and how. If we did this for a gamer named Mary, we could say we had drawn a map of Mary's (version of) gamer affinity space. This "Mary map" will change over time but might well remain reasonably stable for periods.

So imagine Mary is devoted to playing and designing for *The Sims*. We can take a certain period of time—a day, a week, a month, or many months—and map out all the spaces, physical and virtual, and all the routes between them, that Mary uses in pursuit of her interest or passion.

We could make the boundary lines on some spaces and routes on the map thicker than others, based on how much time Mary spends in that space or returns to that space. The thicker the lines, the more time she tends to spend there. We can also, if we like, color-code various spaces and routes based on the sorts of things Mary does in them.

This would be a map of Mary's *Sims* affinity space. The *Sims* affinity space is, of course, one relatively large part of the overall gamer affinity space. And we can draw a Mary map for this, too, if she plays other games as well. The subparts of Mary's *Sims* affinity space—whether they are small parts like her game room at home or larger parts like a gaming convention space (with many rooms) or a fan-based, interest-driven Internet site devoted to *The Sims* (also with many virtual rooms)—are affinity spaces within Mary's overall *Sims* affinity space.

Now take the map we have made for Mary. It is, in some respects, unique to Mary. Certainly her moment-by-moment pattern of movement and activity is unique. But if we compare Mary's *Sims* affinity space to other people's *Sims* affinity spaces, we will find that they more or less overlap with Mary's. The set of people who have a significant overlap with Mary's map constitute a squishy (not rigidly bounded or defined) group. I called this group *fellow travelers* in the preceding chapter. Fellow travelers vary with time and circumstances, and some are together longer than others. It's fluid.

Mary interacts with (or, at least, has ample opportunity to interact with) these fellow travelers. However, anyone who has been in any one of the spaces in her larger *Sims* affinity space is in a yet larger and more amorphous group with Mary. These are people we called *affines*. Even though Mary sees some of these people rarely, any given interaction might be significant and, so, nobody can be discounted. Frequency of contact is not the only significant variable here.

Mary, of course, can traverse different—even many different—affinity spaces, and some of these might have close relationships to one another. For example, Mary may journey in the *Sims* gaming affinity space and in a Photoshop affinity space. These two affinity spaces might be closely related for Mary because she both plays *The Sims* and Photoshops images from *The Sims* for graphic fan fiction. She may, then, also be in a *Sims* fan fiction affinity space and maybe, too, a more general fan fiction affinity space. In two or more of these affinity spaces Mary may have some of the same fellow travelers.

It might also be that one specific interest-driven website—for example, TSR Workshop (www.thesimsresource.com/workshop/)—is so central to Mary's *Sims* endeavors that we can focus on and study it alone as the heart and soul of her endeavors in affinity space, though still tracing where Mary comes from to get there and where she sometimes goes from there (or is led to). We have called such sites *home bases*. People could have several home bases, or none, and some can be physical and others virtual. In Figure 11.1, I sketch out some of the spaces a person might inhabit and travel among in the much larger *Sims* affinity space.

AN EXAMPLE: ALEX AND *THE SIMS* FAN FICTION

Today, many young people get important skills from their travels in affinity spaces. As one example, consider a 15-year-old girl named Alex (Gee & Hayes, 2010). Alex, who we met earlier, has a large following as a fan fiction writer. She uses *The Sims* to create graphic vampire romance stories (images with text). Alex has to make her own images (using tools that can modify images from the game and other tools from outside the game), write and edit (with help from fans) her own texts, and maintain a web presence to keep contact with her thousands of readers. TSR Workshop is one of her home bases, and her own website is a home base for an affinity space organized around her that her devoted fans occupy.

In her work across the many spaces in which she carries out her passion, Alex has learned the following skills at a mastery level (Note: Many of these are no longer necessary to create stories in *The Sims 3* and *Sims 4*. Alex originally used the in-game story mode but later switched to posting stories on her own website, so I will use the latter as the basis for this list):

- Knows *The Sims* as a piece of software inside and out
- Knows in-game design tools and Adobe Photoshop thoroughly
- Created and maintains a very good and highly trafficked personal website
- Knows how to link website and stories to other Sims fan sites to create a network
- Knows how to make custom characters, events, and environments (this requires knowing how to import into Photoshop, use Photoshop editing tools, and save files, then import back into the game)

Figure 11.1. Some of the Spaces in the *Sims* Affinity Space

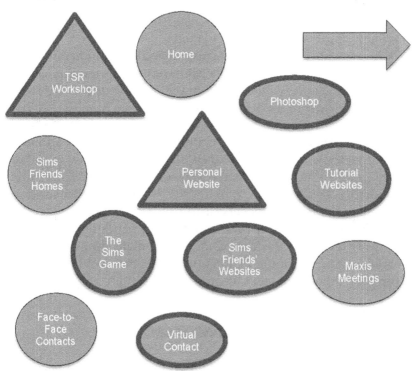

Shapes with thick borders are virtual; those with thin borders are physical. Triangles are home bases. The arrow means that Photoshop is part of a bigger Photoshop affinity space as well.

- Has mastered different sorts of custom software designed by other players
- Knows how to use "cheats" to change or remove unwanted in-game features
- Knows how to access tutorials for various skills as needed and how to design and build a tutorial for others
- Knows how to write compelling narrative
- Knows how to match compelling images with text
- Knows how to recruit readers (i.e., where to advertise her stories, how to create banners as advertisements, "teasers," etc.)

- Knows how to edit and stage her story images (i.e., shading, cropping, etc.)
- Knows how to post text and images on her website to recruit new readers and motivate old ones
- Knows how to respond to fans, especially emotionally, and how to connect them into a community (this requires a style of language very different from the one she uses in her stories)
- Knows how to work with volunteer editors from her fan base

So Alex traverses her own *Sims* affinity space (with her affines and fellow travelers). And she is, as well, the attractor of her own "Alex affinity space," much as Stephanie Meyer, author of the famous vampire romance *Twilight* books, is of her site, but on a smaller scale.

Many of her teenage readers clearly adore Alex and find her deeply helpful in dealing with their problems in being teen girls in the modern world. I base this comment on the emails Alex receives from her readers. She is gaining 21st-century skills that would be the envy of any good school not beset by our current test prep regime.

GOATS AND FARMS

I now want to discuss some important properties of affinity spaces and important reasons to study them. My wife and I recently acquired a small farm. As I neared retirement, I wanted to be able to raise animals and live closer to nature. We were inspired to act when we visited a beautiful goat farm in a small town in Northern Arizona and learned about goats, goat's milk, and making cheese from goat's milk.

As we started our journey we were about as incompetent as you could get. We were true naive newbies. But as adults, we did know something about how affinity spaces work. We knew how to get to some spaces that would help us begin and offer us routes to other spaces and, thus, to a journey, the sort of journey I am calling *development*.

We want to be "real famers"—that is, people who are "into it" and can help their land and animals thrive. We surely do not expect to be masters. Right now we are what I called *laypeople* earlier—in this case, "lay farmers." We hope, however, to eventually join the lowest ranks of the "clergy."

Figure 11.2 sketches out just the part of the goat affinity space we have so far discovered. Since we have gotten not just goats but also pigs, sheep, donkeys, and chickens as well, we are moving "up" to the

Figure 11.2. Spaces in an Affinity Space Devoted to Goats

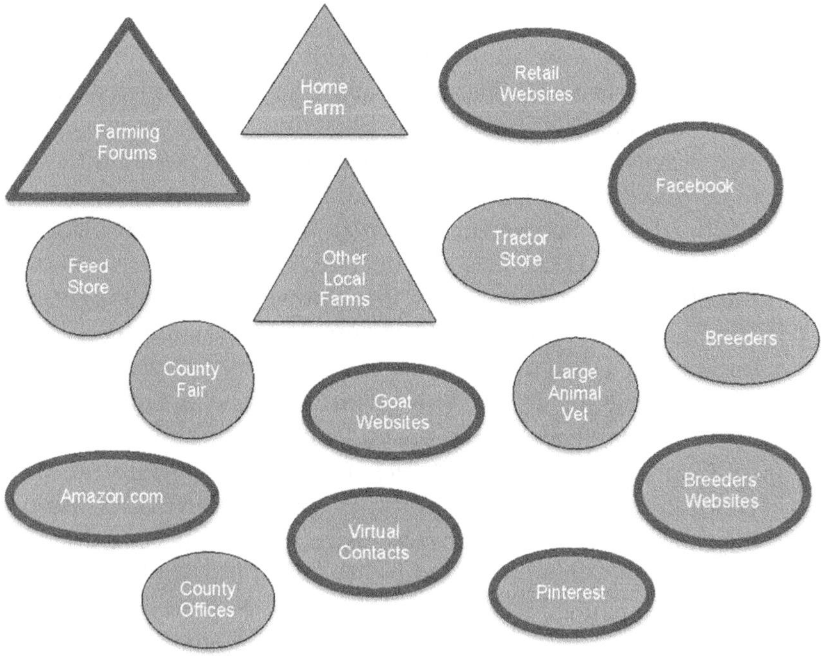

Here are some of the spaces in an affinity space devoted to goats that my wife and I, as new farmers with goats, inhabit. It is how we are learning to be farmers.

larger small-farm affinity space and "down" to donkey, chicken, and sheep affinity spaces.

The piece of affinity space depicted in Figure 11.2 is part of what I have called a distributed teaching and learning system. And, indeed, it is how we are currently being taught and learning (as we engage in doing) to be farmers. Affinity spaces like the ones we have discussed so far (e.g., gamer affinity space, *The Sims* gamer affinity space, fan fiction affinity space, goat affinity space, farm affinity space) have the following important properties:

1. They are repositories of teachers, mentors, more advanced peers, resources, texts, tools and technologies, knowledge, and judgment systems (values, norms, and knowledge about what to do, when to redo, what it is good to do next, and how

to judge what is a good, bad, or a "good enough" result). This is why they can serve as distributed teaching and learning systems.

2. Because they store all the stuff in (1), they are also distributed knowledge systems. They store and transform knowledge. They are repositories of both explicit and tacit knowledge. This is why access to them is consequential. It is very difficult to get the knowledge they store and transform in any nearly as effective and powerful way without access to them. This is why classrooms can be so ineffective. They are rarely part of the affinity space that "owns" the knowledge being taught.

3. They are often repositories of diversity, in the collective-intelligence sense of people with significantly different lived experiences in life. This diversity can be leveraged for collective intelligence. For example, early on in our journey as small farmers we went to "chicken school" in a feed store. This was a 2-hour session that introduced us to the very beginning of what we needed to know to raise chickens successfully.

The space included children, young adults, and older adults. It included raw beginners, people further along, and experts who had come to help (or keep the other experts "honest"). It included well-off people, poor people, and people in between. It included different ethnic groups, including, of course, Mexican Americans (this is Arizona, after all). It included people who had farms, people who wanted to raise chickens at home, and people with all sorts of different jobs and levels of education. The attendees had come to live in Arizona from many different places, they held different political views, and they had lived quite different sorts of lives.

The fact that chicken school was held in a feed store gave us immediate contacts to other spaces, thanks to people from the store, the people teaching the class, the other people in the class, and the store's bulletin board, all of them founts of information about where to go next.

Chicken school was made up of overt instruction (short lectures as we sat on hay bales), participation, discussion, sharing, and things to read and do. Here, truly, was a school inside an affinity space pointing in all sorts of directions to other spaces where more teaching, learning, and development could go on.

PILLAGING AND PLUNDERING

Let's play a game. Below are the names of some "spaces" or things that might be found in them. Can you guess what affinity space they are a part of? Do you know enough about this affinity space to organize them as parts and wholes with routes between them?

Anonymous offshore shell companies
Mossack Fonseca (name of a law firm)
Assets management companies
Wealth management companies
Clandestine Ltd (name of an anonymous offshore company)
Nominee shareholders
Nominee directors
Bearer shares
Beneficial owner
Rossiya Bank (a Russian bank)
Online reputation management company
Compliance department
Dresdner Bank Lateinamerika (a German bank)
Global crisis management firms
British Virgin Islands
Panama
the Bahamas
Bermuda
Samoa
Uruguay
Hong Kong
Nevada
Wyoming
Delaware
Exclusive private banks
VIP departments in major banks

A number of major leaks uncovered by investigative journalists around the world—most recently in what have come to be called the Panama Papers—has thrown light on this secretive affinity space (Obermaier & Obermayer, 2016). In 2015 a source somehow got ahold of the internal database of a major Panamanian law firm named Mossack Fonseca. Mossack Fonseca specializes in setting up anonymous offshore shell companies. The source turned over this data to journalists in Germany who worked for *Suddeutsche Zeitung*, a German newspaper. It was the largest such leak of information ever and included the private records of 214,000 offshore companies, named in 11.5 million documents delivered digitally, totaling 2.6 terabytes of data. Four hundred journalists from all over the world had worked on the data.

Offshore shell companies are used by wealthy people for a variety of purposes. Criminals, such as gunrunners, human traffickers, and drug lords, use them to launder their ill-gotten money. The rich and famous use them to avoid taxes they owe. Politicians and dictators use them when they want to hide their wealth abroad because they have obtained it unethically or illegally, such as in plundering their country's wealth for themselves and their friends and family. Companies use them to hide slush funds from which they draw money for bribes and other sorts of illegal purposes.

Offshore shell companies also have other uses, some of them legal. They are set up by law firms like Mossack Fonseca in Panama, one of the largest such firms in the world, with offices all over the globe. To hide their wealth, to steal from their own countries, to avoid taxes, or to hide their unsavory doings, the rich (or their assistants) move across a great many spaces, physical and virtual.

This offshore shell company affinity space is made up of spaces such as banks, investment firms, consultants, and countries that open, sustain, manage, protect, and hide shell companies, wealth, and the true identities of the shell companies' real owners. Shell companies are most often established in tax havens, places willing to help the rich hide their wealth, criminals carry out their crimes, and dictators pillage their own countries. Some of these tax havens are mentioned in the list above.

This offshore shell company affinity space stores knowledge, judgment systems, resources, and tools, as well as teachers, mentors, advisors, and enablers. It is thus, too, a distributed teaching and learning system, though one to which people like me, and probably most of my readers, have no access. This lack of access, it turns out, greatly limits our ability to harm the world, though it does increase our tax burden.

How consequential is this system? After all, it removes money from countries through tax evasion and other crimes. Here are just a few quotes from the major investigation of the rich and powerful and their offshore shell companies uncovered in the Panama Papers.

According to the British author and *Financial Times* correspondent Tom Burgis, you ought to imagine what's happening in Africa like this: an invisible machine is working to plunder the continent. A looting machine. A coalition of corrupt dictators, unscrupulous large corporations and ruthless banks, all working hand in hand, united by their greed. Mossack Fonseca is a key cog in this machine (Obermaier & Obermayer, 2016, p. 192)

Nicholas Shaxson [a British journalist and investigator] also writes that the offshore world is the "biggest force for shifting wealth and power from poor to rich in history." (Obermaier & Obermayer, 2016, p. 192)

In April 2016 something . . . hidden in plain sight was exposed. Namely that the secret offshore industry—centred in tax havens like the British Virgin Islands—was not, as had been previously thought, a minor part of our economic system. Rather, it *was* the system. Those who dutifully paid their taxes were, in fact, dupes. The rich, it turned out, had exited from the messy business of tax long ago. (Obermaier & Obermayer, 2016, p. xvii)

So affinity spaces need not be benign. They can do great good and they can do great harm. This is so because they are powerful ways to store knowledge and resources and to teach, mentor, and develop people in certain ways. Thus, too, it is crucial to study affinity spaces if we want to understand the world, protect ourselves, and, perhaps, change the world for the better. The study of affinity spaces should be an important part of anyone's education.

A NEW TYPE OF ARCHITECT

We can imagine that there will be—that there should be, at least—a new type of "architect," what I will call an "affinity space architect." An affinity apace architect would be an architect of interest and passion in melded physical and digital spaces in the service of building new types of schools and other teaching and learning spaces. They would be designers and builders of affinity spaces.

Such an architect will consider, based on a given passion as an attractor, all the physical and digital spaces currently available in the world today and the new ones we need to design and build to supplement them, so that we can engage the sorts of teaching, learning, and development we need to make the world a better place. An affinity space architect's goal would be to transform interest and passion in the name of participation, interaction, making, and teaching and learning, for better, more equitable, smarter, more moral, and resilient people, groups, and societies.

The weakness of today's "out-of-school" affinity spaces is often not in their digital spaces and routes (which are copious), but in their physical spaces. Face-to-face embodied communication is primordial and foundational for humans and will never be replaced, unless and until we become a different species altogether. How do we meld good physical spaces and good virtual spaces in the name of learning and transformation? This is a major question for our future.

An affinity space architect must know both material (physical) "stuff" (materials and buildings) and virtual "stuff" (digital and social media and virtual worlds). The affinity space architect must always realize that the social worlds of affines and fellow travelers start with "Mary," that is, they start with individual people who need fellow travelers and affines for their full development and flourishing in the world. Architects have always been experts on how people feel in and move through space, and act and interact in spaces. Today spaces are physical and virtual and melded. And today, melded systems of physical and virtual spaces and routes between them enable the journeys we call development.

CHAPTER 12

Who Are We?

YOU ARE A ZOO: THE HUMAN MICROBIOME

Different areas of research on the brain and the body are converging to show that that we humans are quite different creatures from what we think we are. This research has profound consequences for health, learning, and society at large. So far, it has played next to no role in education and educational policy. While this research is really just at its beginning stage, it will offer up a good many surprising findings in the future. It is something to which people interested in education and development need to pay attention.

We think of our bodies as "ours." We think we are individuals made up of "our" cells, which contain "our" genes. However, virtually every part of the human body—inside and out—harbors a massive zoo of microorganisms, tiny organisms like viruses, bacteria, fungi, and protozoa (Mayer, 2016; McAuliffe, 2016; Moss, 2013; Warner, 2013; Yong, 2016). A typical person contains one hundred trillion of these organisms. If you put them all together, they would outweigh the brain.

The number of microbial cells in our bodies dwarfs the number of our human cells 10 times over. The genetic material of the microorganisms in us is 150 times larger than our human genetic material. What this means is that 90% of the cells we carry around are not us.

But, then, who are "we"? The microorganisms in us affect our physical and mental health, emotions, and behavior. Each of us, depending on all sorts of factors, has a unique set of microorganisms. And we need them to flourish. So in a sense "you" are a zoo; you are a zooey mixture of human and microbial cells. It is this zoo that interacts with the environment and other people, not just "you." It is this zoo that evolves, not human bodies alone. The technical name for this zoo is the *human microbiome*.

While there are massive numbers of microorganisms all over the human body—in every crevice, corner, and organ—the majority of them are in the gut. Unless we are sick, we don't think much about our guts and we certainly don't think very highly of them. It's all a rather embarrassing area, especially compared with the great dignity we accord our brains. But there is something else in your gut that you probably don't know about: a "second brain."

Humans have a nervous system in between the layers of their guts (Mayer, 2016; McAuliffe, 2016; Yong, 2016). This nervous system contains a great many million nerve cells, more than are in the spinal cord. This second brain is in constant communication with the brain in your head via the vagus nerve, the longest of the cranial nerves, extending from the brainstem to the abdomen by way of multiple organs, including the heart, esophagus, and lungs. Ninety percent of the information transmitted by the vagus nerve goes from the gut to the brain, not the other way around, as had previously been thought. These two brains—the head brain and the gut brain—deeply and reciprocally influence each other.

We have receptors all over our bodies that respond to signals from the microorganisms in us or to the chemical products they produce inside us. For instance, certain microorganisms influence the production of serotonin, a chemical that affects how much we eat, how well we sleep, how we feel, and our overall sense of well-being. In the other direction, when we are under stress, our brains release stress hormones (e.g., adrenaline) into our bodies, and these hormones can cause some of the microorganisms in our gut to behave more virulently than they normally do and cause physical and psychological harm to us throughout our bodies.

The microorganisms in the gut aid in digestion, they synthesize vitamins, and they counter the effects of dangerous bacteria. But they also produce nearly every major neurotransmitter that can affect our emotions. And they produce hormones that can affect our psychological health for better or worse. How we feel and behave, and the state of our mental health, are determined not just by our head brain but also by our gut brain. In reality, they are determined by the interactions of our two brains with each other and with our environment.

Dr. Emeran Mayer, director of the Oppenheimer Family Center for Neurobiology of Stress at the University of California, Los Angeles, carried out a study that shows strikingly how the gut brain can influence the states of the head brain (Mayer, 2016). Thirty-six healthy women were divided into three groups. One group ate a commercially available yogurt containing probiotics (bacteria that have a positive effect on the intestines) twice a day for 4 weeks. Another group ate a dairy product that looked and tasted like the yogurt but contained no probiotics. The third group ate no dairy product—yogurt or otherwise—during the 4 weeks.

Before and after the study, subjects were given brain scans to test their responses to images of facial expressions—happiness, sadness, anger, and so on. Mayer found—to his own surprise—that effects from the probiotic yogurt could be seen in many areas of the brain, including those involved in sensory processing and those associated with emotion. For example, he found that the women who ate the yogurt reacted more calmly to the images of different facial expressions than did the two control groups. The bacteria in the yogurt changed the makeup of the yogurt eaters' gut microorganisms and, in turn, this led to the microorganisms' producing chemicals that modified the women's brain chemistry.

What we eat and how we live heavily affect the composition and products of the zoo in our guts. There are better and worse zoos to have. People with healthy diets have a different zoo from that of people with less healthy diets. We now know that diet has an effect not only on their metabolism but also on how they feel and how their brains function (Mayer, 2016; Yong, 2016). Furthermore, certain microorganisms that thrive on unhealthy diets make us want to eat more of the unhealthy diet and lead to obesity, mental and emotional effects, and more bad microorganisms.

The microorganisms that inhabit us—that, in large part, compose us—are sometimes good, even essential, for our well-being. Sometimes they are bad for us, and sometimes they are a bit of both. Furthermore, as we have seen above, stress can turn some of the good ones into bad ones by changing the expressions of their genes.

One example of microorganisms that can do real harm (though not always) are parasites, microorganisms that live in us and derive their nutrients at our expense. Such microorganisms can cause quite an array of effects when they join our zoo. Take, for example, toxocariasis, a parasitic disease caused by the larvae of two species of roundworms whose original hosts are dogs and cats (McAuliffe, 2016). Once in our bodies, these larvae can wander far beyond the gut to other organs such as the liver, lungs, eyes, and even brain. Children infected with this parasite score lower on many cognitive measures such as mathematical ability, reading comprehension, verbal digit recall, visuospatial reasoning, and IQ. This is true even when other factors that are known to depress children's school performance are controlled for (e.g., socioeconomic status, ethnicity, and levels of lead in the blood).

This parasite's harm is, however, not evenly distributed across different groups of people. Thanks to adverse environmental conditions, 23% of African American children are infected with this parasite, in contrast to 13% of Mexican American children and 11% of White children. Educators are well aware that poverty and bad schools cause educational failure, but so can parasites in our guts and heads. There are times—more than we like to think—when a child having problems with reading does not need a reading intervention but a health intervention, not just because of parasites but also because of the overall composition of their zoo and the degree of stress under which they live.

Parents, teachers, and educators know that they are responsible for the well-being and education of children as individuals. But they do not yet fully realize that they are responsible for the well-being and education of children as zoos. How a child feels, thinks, and develops—and the health of the child's mind and body—is heavily influenced by the state of the zoo within the child (the child's own cells and the massive number of microorganisms that accompany them).

We can make children's zoos better or worse. Good nutrition (e.g., a diet not based solely on industrial food), good experiences, a healthy environment, and a sense of well-being can lead to a good zoo (Moss, 2013; Warner, 2013). Bad nutrition and stress can lead to a bad zoo. When we treat the 10% of the child that is "human" and not the whole zoo, we are not treating the whole child.

As I pointed out in Chapter 1, science is really just beginning to study the head brain, the gut brain, our different microbial zoos, and the interactions between these. Much remains to be discovered, and important new results will come fast and furiously.

I also mentioned in Chapter 1 that recently the neurosurgeon James Doty (2016) has argued that we have a third brain, the heart. Like the gut, the heart communicates constantly to the head brain (also via the vagus nerve) and can readily change the state of our head brain and body. Both the gut brain and the heart brain send more communications to the head brain than the head brain sends to them.

Today education is all about the head brain. But educating the head brain does not work well unless we pay attention to guts, hearts, and bodies as well.

YOU ARE A FARM: IDENTITIES

I have argued in earlier chapters that humans can take on different identities. We are not, as far as identity goes, one thing but many. These identities, as we have also said, are not just "in" us. They represent a reciprocal and interacting relationship with social groups and even with history. You cannot be a mime if there are no other mimes. You cannot be a "real mime" if other real mimes do not recognize you as a real mime. You cannot learn to be a mime if you have no access to the values, norms, and activities of mimes.

Our different identities, much like the microorganisms in us, interact with and influence each other. Our identities determine (in part) how we feel, interact with others, think, and believe, and what we value, in different contexts and situations in life. Our identities are like a farm we manage. The health of the farm depends on having healthy identities and ones that "get along" with each other and supplement each other. My identity as a gamer supplements and informs my identity as an academic and vice versa. This is a marriage made in heaven, but only because I have never listened to people who wanted to trivialize my gamer identity or argue that academics can't be "real gamers."

However, too often schools and other segments of society essentialize some identities, such as being African American, a woman, or a person with ADHD, and ignore others that are, at times, just as important or more so, identities such as being a mime, an activist, a gamer, a citizen scientist, or a fan fiction writer. As I argued earlier, it is diversity at the sublevels of identities (at the level of types of women or gamers) that constitute the diversity that is at the heart of collective intelligence.

What makes being an African American, a woman, or a gamer significant is not just the label as a general classification but the different sorts of lived experiences different sorts of African Americans, women, and gamers have had. African Americans, women, and gamers contribute to the essential pool of diversity, not because all African Americans, women, or gamers are the same but because they constitute multiple variations on a theme. Paying attention to the theme and not the variations is a big mistake. In the end, it is the variations that constitute, continually transform, and enliven the theme.

In a classroom, we are not educating "Mary" or "an African American"; we are educating a child named Mary who is a biological zoo and an identity farm. Mary's zoo and farm are unique, not because she is a zoo and a farm (we all are), but because what is in her zoo and on her farm is a unique mixture, especially when we get down to the specifics of types of types.

Mary—and each of us—is unique as a "complex system" (interacting mind brains, gut brains, heart brains, bodies, cells, microorganisms, and socially reciprocating identities) and not merely as an "individual." Mary is as complex as the universe. It is Mary's specific lived experiences of being an African American of a certain sort, for example, and the ways these experiences have informed and been informed by all the other residents of her own zoo and farm that make Mary who she is. They give her gifts to offer that no one else has, if she has been helped and allowed to flourish.

We most certainly need to vigorously fight oppression—oppression in the sense of the denial of the rights and dignity of people with certain identities. We need to fight oppression for just the same reason we need to fight to save diversity in our environment. Denying Mary her full right to be all of what she is, all of what she can become, and all of what she will want to be risks the extinction of something of great value, something that may turn out to be crucial for our world and its survival.

That's how collective intelligence works, how evolution works, how biodiversity works, and how good education should work: The pool of diversity must be kept wide enough to ensure that we, as a species, can adapt, transform, and flourish in the face of change, chaos, and risk. Racism, classicism, and other such *isms* flatten and endanger our shared world. So does essentializing only part of who a person is. So do teaching and tests that standardize, homogenize, and threaten the expression of diverse and promising excellences.

Each of us has many identities, each of which represents a shared and reciprocal relationship with others, not something we have or could have alone. Thus, when we raise or educate any child, we are raising and educating society, all of us, because we are nurturing the future of the ever-changing networks of identities that compose our societies and our world.

When we raise or educate any child poorly—when his or her zoo or farm is impaired or imperiled by a lack of resources, care, or trust—we endanger all of us, because we are endangering the pool of possibilities we humans can use to face our very complex, high-risk, and fast-changing future as a species and, indeed, as a world.

THE HEAD BRAIN

We have seen that how we feel, think, and behave is influenced by the communications between our gut brain and head brain (Mayer, 2016; McAuliffe, 2016; Yong, 2016). In addition, we have argued that how we think, feel, and behave is also a product of our reciprocal relationships with social groups that constitute our identities, identities that shape and constrain us in specific contexts of action and interaction.

We think of our head brains as making "our" decisions, freely chosen. Indeed, we apportion praise and blame on this basis. But our guts and our identities play a role as well. We do not go it "alone." However, there is more: Our head brains do not work the way we think they do. Here, too, it is hard to say who we really are (Bergen, 2012; Buonomano, 2011; Damasio, 1995, 1999; Gazzaniga, 1988, 2011; Hood, 2012; Kahneman, 2011; Macknit & Martinez-Conde, 2010; Marcus, 2008; Renfrew, 2009; Tomasello, 2014).

When we see a snake and jump, we believe we first saw the snake, became afraid, and then jumped. But lots of research over the years has shown that this is not an accurate depiction (Gazzaniga, 2011; James, 1884; LeDoux, 1998). The order in which things actually occurred was this: First, there was an automatic nonconscious reaction to fear, fear set into play by the firing of the amygdala, an almond-shaped set of neurons in the brain linked to both fear responses and pleasure. However, the mind is not yet consciously aware of what triggered the fear. Second, in response to the fear I jumped. Third, I became consciously aware there was a snake there (a relatively slow process compared to feeling fear and reacting).

Most of what goes on in the mind is unconscious and not even open to conscious awareness. We are utterly unaware at any conscious level that the real order was fear-jump-recognize-snake. All I have, at the level of consciousness, to work with here is the after-the-fact information that I saw a snake and that I jumped. The conscious brain does not register that I jumped before I was consciously aware of the snake. Humans are driven by a deep need to make sense of things, often in terms of causality. So I "confabulate" a story that my having seen the snake caused me to jump (when, in fact, my fear and jumping caused me to become consciously aware of the snake).

The human mind/brain is made up of many modules (sets of interconnected neurons) that engage in different tasks. Each module uses sensory inputs from the world and inputs from other parts of the brain and the rest of the body (including, of course, the gut). Each module uses these inputs to make decisions about things like what to feel and desire, how to act and react, to fight or flee in the face of threat, and what is "out there" in the world.

The workings of these modules are not open to our conscious awareness. They are "encapsulated" from consciousness (Gazzaniga, 1988, 2011). The modules pass along their decisions, but not the bases ("evidence") on which they reached their decisions, to a part of our conscious brain we can call "the interpreter." The interpreter has only this information and other things we have consciously seen or know to work with.

The interpreter is driven to seek explanations and causes when, in fact, it very often has only imperfect and quite partial evidence with which to work. It does not know most of the mental processing that went on to make decisions and motivate feelings and actions. The human urge for meaning and casualty drives our interpreters to make up satisfying stories. These stories are often wrong in reality, but they feel so right to us that we are often confident that they are right.

The interpreter has been well studied in neuroscience. What follows is one very telling example among many of how the interpreter works, examples that should worry us. In a well-known 1980 experiment, researchers used makeup to apply a scar to the faces of their subjects and had them look at themselves in a mirror (Kleck & Strenta, 1980; see also Gazzaniga, 2011). Then the researchers told the subjects they were interested in how other people would react to them and their scar in a face-to-face discussion. They asked the subjects to note any behaviors that they thought were reactions to the scar. Just before the discussion started, one of the researchers said he had to moisturize the scar to prevent it from cracking and without the subject's knowledge, he removed the scar.

After the discussions, the subjects were asked how they felt things had gone. They reported that they had been treated badly, because of their scars. When shown a video of the discussion, they would readily stop the tape whenever the other person looked away and attribute this behavior to the person's adverse reaction to the scar.

The subjects used their interpreters to reach an easy, but wrong, explanation. That explanation was based on the information that was consciously available to them, namely, their scar and the other person's frequently looking away. They did as we humans always do, they attributed an effect (looking away) to a cause (the scar).

Research in linguistics on conversation has shown that we all regularly avert our gaze in conversations (Doherty-Sneddon & Phelps, 2005; Gazzaniga, 2011; Kendon, 1967). One reason we do this is that it is harder for listeners to interrupt us when we are not looking directly at them. People also tend to look away when they are mentally engaged in planning what to say next while at the same time finishing what they are currently trying to say. We all do this, but we are rarely ever consciously aware that we do it or when we are doing it.

In the experiment, the fact that the subjects' conversational partners frequently looked away only made it into the subjects' conscious awareness because they were primed to look for suspicious reactions to the scar they thought they had. The subjects told themselves and the researchers a story that made sense based on what the subjects knew, but it was nonetheless wrong. They had no scar, and people frequently look away in conversation for reasons few people are consciously aware of.

This example is typical of something sociolinguists are well aware of. When people have problems in communicative interactions with other people and these problems are caused by miscommunication, they rarely place blame for the problems on this cause (Gee, 2004; Gumperz, 1982; Scollon & Scollon, 1981). They are not consciously aware of sociocultural differences in how people use language and engage in interaction, differences that can cause mismatches and feelings of being out of sync with others. So they attribute the problem to what they can see and are consciously aware of: the other person. They conclude that the other person is dumb, rude, uncooperative, has an agenda, dislikes them, or anything else that makes sense, but this is very often wrong and, indeed, a fertile source of prejudice.

The irony here is that we think we know ourselves better than others know us. Yet the stories we tell about ourselves about why we do what we do are based on partial evidence, with no real access to many of the real causes. Others often have evidence of things we have said and done over time that may, in some cases, make them tell more accurate stories about us than we tell about ourselves (whether or not we like these stories). Furthermore, they may have less desire to make us feel good than we ourselves do.

WHO ARE WE?

Except in the case of severe mental illness, we believe people have free will, make choices, and bear responsibility for them. But what we think, feel, and do is very often mostly a product of unconscious forces and influences from our bodies, gut brains, identities, social dynamics, and the massive parts of our brain that are shut off from conscious awareness. Let's call all these forces together the *fast system* (Kahneman, 2011).

The fast system evolved to allow humans to respond quickly to the world and to other people. It ensures that we do not have to laboriously think out everything we do. We often don't have time for that, and in any case, it would be far too burdensome to have to think through everything all the time. In the fast system, our microbiome, the interacting unconscious modules of our brains, and our social identities think for us.

The fast system usually works well enough for us to survive and get on with life. But in times of fast change and in the face of great complexity it can lead us seriously awry. In these situations, we need to use our conscious brains and think things through. Let us call this the *slow system*, because it takes time and active work.

The trouble is that our conscious brains are but a small part of us. Worse yet, they do not work all that well. Psychologists have studied a great many "brain bugs" in the conscious brain, bugs that cause us to think poorly (Buonomano, 2011; Chabris & Simons, 2009; Gee, 2013; Hood, 2012; Kahneman, 2011; Macknit & Martinez-Conde, 2010; Marcus, 2008).

I discussed one such bug, namely, confirmation bias, in an earlier chapter. This brain bug causes we humans to pay attention to evidence that supports what we already believe and ignore or misconstrue evidence that does not. Another example: Humans are very poor at thinking correctly about probability. Many people engage in safe sex but sunbathe or go to tanning parlors when the probability of dying from skin cancer is much higher than that of dying from AIDS.

But yet our conscious brain, including our often wrong interpreter, is all we have to make good decisions. It's all we have to try to ensure that our gut brain, head brain, and identities are healthy and doing us good and not harm. But how can we make good choices when we are swamped by unconscious biological, mental, and social forces and our conscious brains are so frail? The answer is, Don't do it alone.

Science has a solution to our problem: Test things, pay attention to the results with respect for how the world reacts back to our tests, collaborate with others to share ideas and evidence, and engage in critical discussions with others where your viewpoints are open to criticism and attempts to falsify them. Science makes thinking a team sport in which people supplement one another's weaknesses. It isn't perfect, but it's a lot better than going it alone.

Science is just a formalization of what humans who want to flourish do. People, if they want to make themselves and the world a better place, need to be what I earlier called committed testers. Committed testers try things out, they pay close and respectful attention to how the world or other people respond, and they engage in critical discussions with others who are different from them, discussions in which they can test and sometimes reconsider their ideas and beliefs in the face of other peoples' (Popper, 1994; Soroush, 2000).

The goal of such critical discussions is not for one party to convert the other. It is not a contest. The goal is for both parties to be able to reflect on and come to a better understanding of their own views, transform them if need be, and perhaps, in some cases, converge a little toward truth as a journey and not a final destination. It isn't perfect, but it is the best chance we have in the face of the complex risks, forces of change, and crises in our modern world.

To live a life in which you flourish and others do too is to engage in a team sport. We need more than ourselves. We need people who play different positions, people who know, believe, and do things differently from the way we do. Then the conscious brain is not so frail. Unfortunately, today, media and social forces too often pull people into echo chambers and ideological ghettos where they interact only with others like themselves (Sunstein & Hastie, 2015).

It is the job of parents, teachers, and mentors to help children become lifelong committed testers. And they need to be committed testers themselves. The job of school, at its best, is to train the conscious mind to think well and be a team player. Such a mind will make better decisions about what to eat, how to interact in the world, and how to seek out environments that make mind and body healthy. And then the fast system and the slow system will work well separately and together. It will never be perfect. But it's the best we can do and a good deal better that what we often currently do: go it alone and stay in like-minded silos with others.

CHAPTER 13

Frameworks and Reflective Discussions

SOCIAL GROUPS AND FRAMEWORKS

Human development, from childhood on, is a fragile process. For us humans, problems always abound and resilience is crucial, but hard. No matter how hard parents, teachers, and mentors work to help raise healthy children into adulthood, the state of the society in which a person lives is a crucial limiting force on healthy development. A bad society can undo a great deal of good developmental processes, whether they occur at home, at school, or in social activities out of school.

Human learning is largely a type of socialization. Humans learn by being embedded in social groups of all different sorts, groups connected to institutions, cultures, communities, interests, and activities. Teachers and mentors in these groups design and mentor learning experiences for "newcomers" young and old. They also, in the process, pass on judgment systems. A judgment system helps learners to know where to start when attempting to accomplish a goal, what a good or bad outcome is from an attempt, how to go on when things do not work out or need redoing, and what the values and standards for an acceptable stopping point are.

Judgment systems are formed and "owned" by social groups with special interests or skills. These groups can be as small as families and local churches and communities and as large as religions and cultures, with a great many sorts of interest-driven and activity-based groups in between, among them mimes, gardeners, gamers, carpenters, media producers, activists, professionals of all sorts (lawyers, doctors, nurses, teachers, scientists), and a great many other kinds of people.

We have seen that pattern recognition is a human superpower and the source of general knowledge and principles. Generalizations are learned bottom-up from many experiences as learners gradually find patterns and subpatterns in their experiences. Here, too, learners need help. It can be hard to find patterns and subpatterns that are actually true and useful for future action.

Furthermore, humans are prone to find false or misleading patterns and to run with them without really testing them. So social groups also guide learners in what count as important and useful patterns and subpatterns in experience, how these translate into general principles, and how to use them in future action and talk.

All this help is a double-edged sword. On the one hand it gives us meaning-making frameworks (perspectives, theories, viewpoints) that guide our thinking and acting (Gee, 2014; Holland et al., 1998; Holland & Quinn, 1987; Strauss & Quinn, 1997). We bring values, norms, generalizations, and characteristic ways of seeing and doing to how we think about, talk about, and act in regard to things and events in the world. We all have different "takes" on (ideas about) such things as parenting, children, cooking, citizenship, morals, gender and sexuality, race, class, friendship, drinking, drugs, marriage, schooling, books, media, play and work, intelligence, strangers, politeness, animals, conservation, the environment, God, and anything and everything else, based on our socialization as learners within social groups.

However, these frameworks can lead to divisive interactions between humans who have different frameworks. Since our frameworks come from enculturation and socialization, we are often not fully consciously aware of them. We have not usually thought much about them in a critical way. Nonetheless, because they have come from our own experiences and from social groups to whom we may be deeply attached, we often cherish our frameworks as part and parcel of who we are and what we stand for.

Whether or not the differing frameworks people in a given society hold—and now across our deeply connected global world—lead to respectful discussions or head-on conflict depends on the state of the society in which a person lives. Difference can be a source of strength and collective intelligence or cause conflict, hatred, and even war.

INDIVIDUALS, SOCIAL GROUPS, AND SOCIETY

There is now a good deal of research that shows that societies that have high levels of inequality are toxic in a great many different ways (Marmot, 2004; Pickett & Wilkinson, 2011; Stiglitz, 2013). Such

societies lead to a lack of respect and caring for others and to difference as source of disdain and hatred. They lead to widespread anxiety
and feelings of low self-worth. They are profoundly detrimental to
healthy development, not just for the poor but for everyone. This is
not a political but an empirical statement.

We all know that poor people fare less well in societies than do
rich people. But what most people do not know is this: In a highly unequal society, all the problems we tend to associate with poverty are
more common *for everyone*—poor, middle-class, and rich. In a highly
unequal society, many well-off people resemble poorer people in less
unequal societies.

The United States today has the highest inequality in its history
(Stiglitz, 2013). Thus, it turns out, everyone in the society is, on average, worse off in terms of well-being than people of their same class in
more equal societies. This means that, on average, even a rich person
in a highly unequal society will be less well off in terms of health and
happiness than a rich person in a less unequal society.

High levels of inequality in a society are toxic to everyone in that
society, across race, class, and gender. Here is a list of negative effects
that are on average all significantly worse for all, not just the poor, in a
highly unequal society than in more equal ones (Pickett & Wilkinson,
2011):

Poorer physical health
More mental illness
Lower levels of child well-being
Lower levels of trust
Less caring for others
Higher levels of obesity
Higher divorce rates
Higher teenage birth rates
More bullying
Lower social mobility
More segregation of rich and poor
Greater prison population
Lower literacy skills
Higher levels of violence

Why should this be so? Why are all people in a highly unequal society, on average, less well off than people in a more equal society? One

reason is there is too much focus on status (Marmot, 2004; Pickett & Wilkinson, 2011). In highly unequal societies people live with a great deal of anxiety about status. They question their self-worth regardless of their position in society. They fear that what they do or think does not really count in and contribute to their society.

Humans have an innate, primordial need to feel a sense of self-worth, to feel that they matter to others and to society, to feel that they are valued participants in their own society. People's sense of self-worth is heavily tied to how they think other people view them. When humans do not feel that they really count, that they are not valued, they get sick in mind and body. When too many people in a society feel this way, the whole society is sick.

In the United States many people seem to have a high regard for themselves but actually do not. Many tend to be deeply insecure and far too focused on how they appear to others. They seem to have an induced type of narcissism in which their insecurity leads them to focus inward on the self and not outward on the needs of other people. By 2006 two-thirds of American college students scored above what had been the average narcissism score in 1982 (Pickett & Wilkinson, 2011).

Real self-worth is based on a realistic sense of competence and on hard work that a person believes will pay off in terms of respect and participation. That is what development and education should be about. But in a highly unequal society, many people seek short-term satisfaction because they do not believe that effort over the long haul will really make any difference for them.

In terms of physical health and rates of anxiety, high inequality affects everyone in a society, not just the poor (who are nonetheless often most affected). In the United States, the poor have shorter lives than the rich, and people who are well off have shorter lives than the very rich. Conversely, it is also the case that as inequality lessens, everyone in society benefits, not just the poor. At any level of income, it is better, all things being equal, to live in a more equal society (Marmot, 2004; Pickett & Wilkinson, 2011; Stiglitz, 2013).

As Sebastian Junger in his book *Tribe: On Homecoming and Belong* (2016) points out,

> Humans don't mind hardship, in fact they thrive on it; what they mind is not feeling necessary. Modern society has perfected the art of making people not feel necessary. (p. xvii)

In his book Junger tells stories of people who found a greater sense of belonging amid disaster than they did living in modern affluent societies. For example, when Serbia attacked Bosnia and laid siege to its capital, Sarajevo, nearly 70,000 people, about 20% of the population, were killed or wounded. People were without food and water and witnessed violence daily. Conditions were horrific. Yet one woman, talking about Bosnia after the war had ended, told Junger:

> I missed being that close to people, I missed being loved in that way, . . . In Bosnia—as it is now—we don't trust each other anymore; we became really bad people. We didn't learn the lesson of the war, which is how important it is to share everything you have with human beings close to you. (pp. 69–70)

When Junger asked this woman if people had ultimately been happier during the war, she said, "We were the happiest, . . . and we laughed more." Junger relates that someone spray-painted on a wall—about the loss of solidarity in Bosnia after the war ended—the slogan "It was better when it was really bad."

Such a phenomenon is far from atypical; researchers have repeatedly found that when humans face an existential crisis from wars or natural disasters, they don't fall apart but pull together. Their health often gets better, and those suffering from mental illness improve. Again, to quote Junger:

> As people come together to face an existential threat, . . . class differences are temporarily erased, income disparities become irrelevant, race is overlooked, and individuals are assessed simply by what they are willing to do for the group. It is a kind of fleeting social utopia that . . . is enormously gratifying to the average person and downright therapeutic to people suffering from mental illness. (pp. 53–54)

This all sounds very odd indeed, but such is the power of the human need to belong, count, and contribute, a need badly impaired not only in highly unequal societies but also too often by affluence and modern life in general. This is not a plea for war, of course, but rather a claim that modern highly unequal societies are a form of war on many people's sense of self-worth and mental health. It is a plea that we see high levels of inequality as an existential crisis for the human spirit and that we get in the same boat together to work our way to a better place for all.

OUR CURRENT SHARED EXISTENTIAL CRISIS

We live today in a world where people with different frameworks, stemming from different families, educational backgrounds, communities, religions, cultures, institutions, and nations, not only disagree with one another but also too often dismiss, denigrate, or even seek to harm others who have different frameworks from theirs. Since people often cherish their own frameworks, they are reluctant to change them or even to discuss them with people who disagree with them for fear they will lose their faith in what they cherish and need.

In a world like the one we live in today, there is a pressing need for teachers who know how to teach people, young and old, to care about and learn from what I will call "reflective discussions" (Popper, 1994; Soroush, 2000). Such discussions involve respectfully discussing differing frameworks on important issues. The goal of such discussions is not to convert other people to "our side." It is not even to reach truth in the short run. The goal is that both parties to such discussions will come—over time—to understand their own frameworks better, be able to argue for them at a conscious level, and may modify parts of them as they learn from others. The goal is also to appreciate the overall shape of other people's frameworks, not just as isolated claims but in the contexts of their lived experiences. The ultimate goal is to test whether people, over time and with goodwill, can gradually converge, even if only partially, on frameworks that lead to a better world for all people, and, indeed, all living things (because all living beings are in this together).

What stands in the way of reflective discussions is the view, common on the political right and left, that the goal of argument is to show someone else that he or she IS wrong (and even stupid or evil). This does not work well as a means to move people closer together and certainly not to recruit them to a common cause. Reflective discussions are based on thinking about truth not as a final destination, which we frail humans will reach any time soon (or even ever), but as a journey where, over the long haul, we may gradually converge on truth or, at least, a better form of life with one another.

Reflective discussions also crucially require that people respect the world in the sense that they seek to test parts or all of their frameworks by acting in the world and paying respectful attention to what the world "says back" to their actions. The world that speaks back to us may be the natural world or the world of other people and social interactions.

Respectful attention to how the world "talks back" means two things: first, asking honestly whether the results the world gives back to our tests (actions followed by reflection) really supports our beliefs and values, and, second, consulting with other people who differ from us in regard to how they assess the world's response to similar sorts of actions. This is just what *evidence* really means, and it is basically the process that science formalizes. Again, the goal is not to prove someone—even yourself—right or wrong, once and for all, but for each of us to improve our frameworks in terms of the quality of our own lives and those of others with whom we share this planet.

If people do not respect the world's responses to their actions and beliefs, they cannot really have a reflective discussion with others, because they are not open to change. And, too, the response of others to us in reflective discussions is also an aspect of the world's "talking back." These others, like us, were developed by the society and world in which we all live. One way or another, their frameworks are reflections of and insights into that society and world.

I am not saying that we should never criticize and never agitate against what we see as error or evil. But we can hardly understand other people's frameworks deeply enough to criticize them if we have not respectfully listened to them and reflected fairly on their frameworks. Furthermore, none of us is in possession of anything like any final truth.

People who have enough goodwill to commit themselves to reflective discussions and to respecting the world and other people's responses to their actions are what I earlier called committed testers. Such people realize that all frameworks and all cultures have flaws. As the Iranian philosopher Abdolkarim Soroush (2000) has said, "Each culture must disavow certain elements of Itself" (p. 167). Soroush also captures well what it means to be a committed tester:

> We can have two visions of reason: reason as destination and reason as path. The first sees reason as the source and repository of truths. The second sees it as a critical, dynamic, yet forbearing force that meticulously seeks the truth by negotiating tortuous paths of trial and error. (pp. 89–90)

COMPARING FRAMEWORKS

Meaningful reflective discussions across different frameworks in science, religion, politics, or culture are not about vetting individual claims (Popper, 1994; Quine, 1951; Soroush, 2000). They are about testing whole frameworks (all the claims in them as interrelated ones) against different ways of talking about and looking at experience.

In a reflective discussion we need to discuss and compare networks of claims that support each other, not a single claim out of the context of its supporting framework. We do not, for example, want to know whether someone thinks abortion is (or is not) murder. Rather, we want to get at the whole network of ideas, values, and knowledge claims in which this belief resides and from which it gets its meaning and support for a given person.

Let me give a specific example of what I mean when I say that we do not test our frameworks claim by claim but in only in terms of a whole set or system of interrelated claims that compose the framework. For years now, one area in which I have worked is on the affordances of video games for good learning (Gee, 2007). I have made the claim that "video games are good for learning" (in and out of school). But this claim is but one part of a set of claims that make up my framework (theory) about games and learning (Gee, 2011). Figure 13.1 presents a simplified picture of my framework.

Figure 13.1. Claims in Frameworks

Video games are good for learning		
Only good games are good for learning	Good = incorporate good learning principles	Learning = situated/sociocultural approach
Good game = Good fit between game mechanics + interesting & challenging problems	Learning principles = from recent research in the learning sciences	Learning = mentored problem solving
Good game design is a form of teaching	Good = when integrated in a learning system, not stand-alone	Learning = problem solving
		Learning requires teaching
		Teaching = well-designed experiences
		Teaching = people, tools, design

When people do research to test my claim that video games are good for learning, they often have the view that science is about testing claims one by one to see if they are "true" or "a fact." But imagine that someone argued that he or she had shown my claim to be false based on evidence from the person's research. My claim is connected to a whole set of other claims. Faced with their evidence, I can change or adjust any one or more of these other claims and keep my claim that video games are good for learning. Perhaps I will say that the game he or she tested was not a "good game." Even if it was, I can modify my definition of *good game*. I can adjust any of my claims or their relationships in my framework in a myriad of ways.

Any statement in my framework could have been shown in bold as the one people wanted to test or discuss, but things would still work the same. Any one statement brings all the others with it, and the results of any test can be spoken to by myriad different adjustments. All we can ever do—in science, religion, politics, or culture—is to honestly look at our frameworks (or have critics do it), draw logical consequences from the claims in our frameworks, and then ask ourselves honestly whether these consequences are good for our purposes and good for the world we share with others.

EVIDENCE, INTERPRETATION, AND REFLECTIVE DISCUSSIONS

I have argued that respect for evidence and engaging in respectful critical discussions are crucial to what I have called becoming a committed tester. However, it is important to understand the crucial role of interpretation in both reflecting on evidence and engaging in critical discussions.

Any evidence we collect and any framework we have has to be put into words if we are to reflect on them and discuss them with others. However, words do not have once-and-for-all fixed meanings. What a word mean varies across different contexts of use, and it is not always easy to figure out what a word means in context. Often we have to work, reflect, and discuss with others in order to figure out what a given word means in a text or in talk. Sometimes, too, we have to negotiate with others what we are all going to mean by a word, or we need to find new words to get past stumbling blocks.

To see my point here more concretely, let's take an example, the word *sausage*. What does this word mean? A dictionary might say something like "Sausage is ground-up meat parts, together with other ingredients, usually stuffed inside a casing of some sort."

Now, at the food store you have to confront applications of the word *sausage* on packages, in ads, and in your own talk and decisions. And, alas, there are lots and lots of different things in sausage (Nerbribk & Borch, 1993)—all sorts of animal body parts, some of which many people (and some government agencies) don't consider to be meat. Here are just a few of the things other than meat that can be in sausage: animal fat, rusk, bread crumbs, cereal, water, polyphosphates, soya, colors, preservatives, sulphates, nitrates, antioxidants, flavor enhancers (e.g., monosodium glutamate), and, of course, a wide variety of contaminates.

U.S. government regulations define meat in such a way that pork sausage, for example, can contain up to 30% fat, 25% connective tissue, as little as 42% meat, and lots of ingredients that no one thinks are meat, and still count both as "meat" and "sausage" (www.sausagelinks. co.uk/sausage-facts/health-legal/). On the other hand, some consumers would beg to disagree.

So consumers, producers, supermarkets, economic markets, government agencies, courts, health groups, and others discuss, contest, and negotiate over what can be said to be "sausage" in actual situations. Consumers do not want sausage to be so "pure" that it is too expensive to buy. Producers want it not so "impure" that consumers die from eating it (because then they can't buy it again) but also not so expensive that they cannot make a good profit. Supermarkets want to keep their customers, but not go broke. Courts are asked things like, "Just how many rat droppings can sausage have in it and not count as sausage any more?" And people from different cooking cultures have different opinions about what can or cannot be in "real" sausage. It's all a mess.

All sorts of people, institutions, and interest groups get involved and help move meanings in different directions through their talk, arguments, actions, interactions, purchases, and cooking. A dictionary settles nothing here on its own. Things change. Some people win and some lose, and this changes, too, across time. Meaning is social and cultural and contestable and practical, even if people share the same dictionary.

As far as I know, no one has gone to war over what is in sausage. However, plenty of people have killed, maimed, and gone to war over what *democracy, Christianity, Islam, White, Black, fair, just, liberal, kin, family, God, honor, clean, pure, male, female, reason, religion, science,* and many other such words—all as messy as *sausage*—mean at the point of their applications to the world. How do people settle arguments other than through hate, war, intolerance, and withdrawing into meaning ghettos?

So this is a different way to look at meaning. Meaning is not something locked away in heads or dictionaries. Meaning is something we negotiate and contest socially. Negotiation and contestation can take place peacefully only when people have goodwill and feel they share a fate with others.

One important context that we need to be consider when we want to know the meanings of words is history. Consider, for instance, the Second Amendment to the U.S. constitution and all the consternation it has caused in regard to guns. The Second Amendment says, "A well regulated militia being necessary to the security of a free state, the right of the people to keep and bear arms shall not be infringed."

In his book *The Second Amendment: A Biography*, Michael Waldman (2014) points out that the world of the Second Amendment at its inception would be unrecognizable to us today. In 1791, when the Bill of Rights was adopted, all White American males served in a state's militia for life. They purchased their own weapons, stored them in their homes, and brought them to battle when they needed to fight.

The Militia Acts, enacted in Congress in 1792, provided for the organization of state militias. At the time there was no federal standing army. The Militia Acts authorized the president to take command of the state militias if invasion or insurrection was imminent. George Washington used this authority in 1794 to suppress the Whiskey Rebellion, a protest on the western frontier against a new federal tax on whiskey (ironically, the whiskey rebels' battle cry was "No taxation without representation," something over which Washington had just fought a war with England).

Today, the militia is gone and the federal army is massive. Not every male is in the National Guard, let alone a militia. And soldiers do not supply their own weapons. So does or does not the Second Amendment say that every American has the right to bear arms? How do we make sense of its original meaning now when its historical context is long gone? How can we construe its meaning for today, and how close does this meaning have to be to its meaning in 1791?

We have a Supreme Court that makes decisions on issues like these, but their decision that the Second Amendment gives everyone the right to bear arms, including military-grade arms, has by no means ended controversy on the matter. For example, after he retired from the court, former chief justice Warren Burger—decrying the power of the gun lobby in the United States—said that the Second Amendment "has been the subject of one of the greatest pieces of fraud—I repeat the word 'fraud'—on the American public by special interest groups that I have ever seen in my lifetime" (Biskupic, 1995, p. A20; see also Younge, 2016).

Words in our critical discussions of frameworks with others need to be interpreted. And that interpretation requires effort, education, and the realization that interpretation is a social—and yes, historical and political—act. The study of language, culture, history, texts, and interpretation should be at the very heart of the education of any citizen in a society that wants to stay both civil and free. The humanities are core to the study of interpretation, but educational reformers have left these disciplines withering in the dust in contemporary America and much of the rest of the world, in favor of STEM (science, technology, engineering, and mathematics). The results are predictable.

CLASHING FRAMEWORKS IN ACTION

I now want to discuss an example of what happens when frameworks clash and there are no reflective discussions to mitigate the event. Years ago I worked in the town of Worcester, Massachusetts. Worcester is a fascinating place. It has been a town since long before the United States became an independent country. For hundreds of years Worcester has defined itself against Boston (the bigger, more prosperous, and more prestigious city near it). In the colonial era, Worcester was free soil (opposed to slavery and the return of escaped slaves), while Boston was much more tepid in these matters.

By the early 20th century Worcester was a successful industrial working-class town. Its population was a mix of 19th-century "White" immigrants (from places like Poland, Russia, Ireland, and other parts of Europe) and African Americans whose families went back to the Underground Railroad (the secret routes and way stations to freedom from slavery). This population "melted" (as in the "melting pot") into "Americans" primarily by becoming common citizens of Worcester first and foremost. Many teachers in Worcester's public schools had used teaching as a way to enter the middle class from working-class family backgrounds.

By the 1970s Worcester's industrial base was beginning to decay, a victim of the outsourcing of jobs. A once vibrant working-class community became financially depressed. Furthermore, the population of Worcester was fast "browning" as a result of a new wave of immigration from Asia, South America, Mexico, and the Caribbean. The teachers in the public schools, themselves a product of immigration, viewed the "Brown" children in their classrooms as "Worcester kids" and felt it was their job to help them become citizens of Worcester, and, thus, in that sense, to "melt," as had their own families.

Worcester has a number of good colleges, and some years ago there was a project in one of them where university history professors and public middle school teachers worked together to design and teach a new history curriculum based on students' engaging in local oral history. I was part of a team facilitating the meetings between the professors and teachers and also involved with studying their discourse practices (Gee, 2014).

The project went on for many meetings and eventually a curriculum was made and taught. However, the meetings were often contentious. From interviews it became apparent that the professors thought the teachers were racists and the teachers thought the professors looked down on them and did not trust them. At one meeting a professor asked a teacher if she had much diversity in her classroom (which was, in fact, made up of White, Asian, South American, Mexican, African American, and Caribbean students). The teacher said, "No, they're all Worcester kids."

The professors wanted the middle school kids to study their own neighborhoods (so, for example, a Vietnamese student would engage in oral history within a largely segregated Vietnamese neighborhood, which not so long ago had been, perhaps, a Polish neighborhood). The teachers wanted students to focus on the downtown of Worcester ("the center") and the people who went there from the socially and culturally diverse neighborhoods of Worcester.

The professors and the teachers never overtly discussed their conflicts or the possible sources of those conflicts. Eventually we noticed, however, that over the course of many meetings, the professors had used the words *diverse* and *diversity* many times but never used words for having things in common. The teachers, on the other hand, rarely used *diversity* but often used terms for having things in common as citizens of Worcester.

It became clear that the professors and the teachers brought two different frameworks to the meetings. Of course, people do not normally formalize their frameworks in explicit claims, and so I cannot know the full details of their frameworks. However, as a discourse analyst, using various sources of data, I can make hypotheses about their frameworks, given how the professors and teachers talked, interacted, acted, and expressed values.

Here are simplified versions of the two different frameworks:

Professors

1. Honoring diversity is the primary goal in schooling.
2. Diversity is defined in terms of race, class, and gender, but with a primary emphasis on race.
3. Stressing commonality over diversity is a form of colonization.
4. Failing to orient to a child's race or ethnicity is a form of racism.
5. Academics have privileged insight into the politics of race and diversity.
6. Larger macrolevel power structures systematically victimize "people of color," thereby severely limiting their agency at a local level.
7. Larger macrolevel power structures are where the important causes and effects actually happen, though most people do not have the insight or knowledge to see this or really understand it.
8. Diverse neighborhoods should be the focus of Worcester, not the downtown, which is possibly unsafe anyway.
9. Teachers and the American public in general are not sophisticated intellectually or politically.
10. Teachers are locally focused; academics are nationally and globally focused.

Teachers

1. Honoring commonality is the primary goal of Worcester public schooling.
2. The earlier "White" immigrants (their own families) "melted" into being co-citizens of Worcester and the new "Brown" immigrants need to do so too.
3. One key goal of schooling is to make students become citizens of Worcester.

4. Placing children in large social groups effaces their individuality.
5. Teachers are there to teach individual children, not "abstract" groups.
6. Class is more central than race or ethnicity in terms of people failing to get ahead.
7. The primary causes of people's success and failure are at the local level and a matter of their individual agency.
8. In a community where new immigrants are poor and often (the teachers believe) have dysfunctional families, teachers must not just teach but also nurture the children as individuals.
9. The downtown of Worcester needs to be a focus for everyone because that is where all the people of Worcester used to come together as citizens of Worcester. It needs to be revitalized.
10. Though college professors teach, they are not teachers.
11. Academics live in an ivory tower and do not know what is happening on the ground.

Note that it will not do much good to pick one claim and ask whether it is true or choose one word and ask what it "really" means. This is so because each claim and each key word is inextricably linked to many of the other claims and words in each framework. It is not surprising that the professors felt the teachers were hiding things or even lying and that the teachers felt the professors looked down on them and attributed racism to them.

What might have happened if the participants in this project had seen the value of a reflective discussion comparing both frameworks in their entirety, with the goal not being to convince one another or settle in any final way a given claim or word meaning? The goal would have been for both parties to come to a better understanding of their own framework, learn better ways to argue for it and explicate what it means, face new questions, and discover what parts of their framework, if any, they wanted to change or reformulate.

Both parties to such a discussion would respect evidence in the sense of how the world reacts to what they do and say when they use their framework in the world. In the end, they would all settle, not for final truth or conversion, but for the possibility that transformed frameworks may gradually evolve and at least partially converge, in the course of critical discussions based on goodwill, toward frameworks that are truer, deeper, and more collaborative in the interest of some common good.

I have said several times that what is required for such critical discussions is goodwill. But now we reach our final question: What could possibly be the source of goodwill in our politically, socially, religiously, culturally, and ideologically fractured country and world? Goodwill is precisely what is often missing in highly unequal societies. I do not know the final answer to this vexed question. I do know this: The place to start is good teachers and good teaching in and out of school.

CHAPTER 14

Conclusion

This is not a book about educational policy. It is about human development. Humans can learn and flourish only under certain conditions. The nature of human development sets the limits for what can work in or out of school, regardless of what policymakers, politicians, publishers, and test-makers try to tell us and sell us. If the viewpoint in this book is even close to the truth, schools, as we know them, are a poor fit with how human beings actually develop. This is why, thanks to new technologies and new forms of participation, new ways of teaching and learning are proliferating out of school.

Schools are the way they are because they are institutions that respond more to politics, business, schools of education, and public divisions over ideology, religion, and culture than they do to the actual needs of real children. Schools are hard to change, especially in a highly unequal society where many people use advantaged schools to accelerate their children's progress toward positions of prominence over other people's children, who are left to inferior schools.

Even when good ideas about learning, development, and technology are brought to school, they often become prey to reformers and businesses seeking to standardize, commodify, and go to scale in the name of profit and efficiency. In the process, the *good* in the good ideas is lost and the core grammar of schooling does not really change.

Both learning and teaching have become ubiquitous in the modern world. They go on in all sorts of institutions, among them museums, libraries, and community centers, and all over the Internet and via social media. Good teaching no longer resides in just one individual called a *teacher*. It now also resides in activity-based social systems and in smart technologies. Teaching today, at its best, involves using multiple good technologies and good forms of social interaction and participation to design good learning experiences so that learners can know, do, and become.

Human beings are frail. Human development is frail. We are conscious creatures—aware of injustice, suffering, and death—but have quite limited self-knowledge (Gee, 2013). Our brains, as we have seen, are full of brain bugs that hamper good thinking, and our guts are full of bugs that, if they are a bad mix, can make us quite unhealthy in mind and body. We humans can be smarter together than apart, but we often have a hard time being together, especially with people who are not like us (which is the vast majority of people on earth).

Processes of socialization and enculturation—the bases of human development—give our lives meaning and bring us a sense of belonging. But they can also divide us into warring tribes of all different sorts. And in the end, we are all victims when the society we live in is highly unequal and unfair. Victims have to fight back. To do that, they need faith in themselves, and they need teachers.

Humans will never be perfect. Institutions—including schools—will never be perfect. Not even close. Beware of those who try to sell perfection. Even if we could redeem every child—and I believe we can—we cannot do it on the same time line for everyone. We can never give up on development, because we can never really know when and how any human, no matter how "behind," "at risk," or "damaged" we think he or she is, will rise up. When things got about as bad as they possibly could have been, the people of Sarajevo rose up fully fit to the challenge (Junger, 2016).

We often hear—quite understandably—the question "What can I do?" What can teachers in schools do in the face of our current testing and accountable regimes? What can a citizen do in a country ruled by money and greed? What can people do in a world awash with poverty, violence, and environmental degradation? As we have discussed in this book, they can do the following:

- Connect and integrate knowing, doing, and being.
- Give learners access to authentic judgment systems connected to valued activities and groups of people who have a passion for these activities. This is what standards really ought to mean.
- Be a tour guide to, and a curator and aggregator of, the interests and passions in and out of school that matter, and engage people in the world (some of these are in the "real world," some are on the Internet or social media, and some are in both places).

- Design and mentor good +experiences (where there is action to take, learners care about the outcome of the action, and they are helped to manage their attentional resources). Connect learners to other mentors.
- Team up and work with other teachers, adults, and learners (in the real world and on the Internet) to design and revise good learning experiences in and out of school. As a teacher, become your own educational reformer.
- Model for learners what to pay attention to and how to manage one's attention in a learning experience, and model how to talk about and reflect on one's former experiences and one's vicarious experiences from books, and from media of all other sorts, for making sense, preparing for future action, and making good choices.
- Be a dialogic talker engaging learners one-on-one and in small groups, as well as in larger groups, with different varieties of language (including academic and specialist varieties of language) used appropriately for different situations, for different purposes, and in different genres. Talk about your own experiences, real and vicarious, and your own learning and problem solving. And talk about how talk, thinking, and texts work as systems and in the world—that is, regularly go "meta."
- Let learners sample, study, and reflect on the wide variety of different language, literacy, and media practices at work in the world, with a special focus on language and media awareness, that is, learning how communication works for good and ill, and in transparent and hidden ways, in society and the world. Be sure that learners learn a repertoire of language, literacy, and media skills fit for different purposes and collaborations.
- Place literacy activities and skills within the larger ecologies of activities of all different (multimodal) sorts that give any specific literacy activity or skill its meaning, power, and possible good or bad effects in the world.
- Develop learners as proactive agents, deliberate learners (self-teachers), complex thinkers with insight, and good choosers.
- Teach collective intelligence—that is, teach how diversity, smart tools and technologies, and people with different skill sets but shared goals, can solve hard problems and be smarter than any one person could be alone.

- Honor all the identities every learner has, including activity-based identities, but always be aware of the complex relations people can have with even their own identities and how each of us is—or should be—a "riff" on an identity and not contained by it.
- Encourage learners to see failure as good for learning and as a form of exploration, and even encourage them to invite it on the way to making progress.
- Know when to let learners play and muck around and do not make a fetish of time, speed, or success.
- Remember that humans are frail. Their brains have many bugs (e.g., confirmation bias), people are not conscious of a good deal of why they feel and act as they do, and high levels of stress can make individuals very sick. Teach learners that they do not have to go it alone and should readily "plug into" and play (work) with other people and good tools and technologies in a spirit of discovery.
- Help learners become committed testers, that is, people who actively look to challenge or test their own beliefs and who respect evidence in the sense of paying attention to and honoring the feedback they get from the world and from others when they act and interact.
- Teach learners, as committed testers, to engage in critical discussions in which they can compare, contrast, argue for, and discuss different frameworks (connected sets of perspectives, assumptions, theories, and ideas), not just single claims, in the spirit, not of conversion or condemnation, but of mutual understanding and possible transformation of one's own frameworks.
- Remember that humans are zoos: They are complex beings made up of self and a microbiome of other creatures. Each of us has a head brain, a gut brain, and a heart brain in constant communication with one another and with our microbiome and the physical and social environments through which we move and in which we act.
- Remember that humans are identity farms. They develop, nourish, and sometimes struggle with multiple identities tied to their activities, affiliations, and allegiances in (and imposed by) the world and to affordances and constraints the world gives them.

- The best way to make healthy humans (both as zoos and as farms) is to make them feel that what they do really matters, that they count, and that they can actively participate in and have something important to offer society. This is also the best way—in fact, it is the only way—to make a healthy society.

In the end, no matter how constrained and harassed any teacher is, if he or she makes any child feel as though the child authentically counts, matters, and belongs, the teacher has kept the long battle for human dignity going. And to do this, teachers need to know, feel, and demand that *they too* count, matter, and belong at the heart of education. We will never know if the destination is reachable unless we start and continue on the journey.

References

Ackerman, D. (2005). *An alchemy of mind: The marvel and mystery of the brain.* New York, NY: Scribner.

Adams, M. J. (1990). *Beginning to read: Thinking and learning about print.* Cambridge, MA: MIT Press.

Aguilar, E. (2016). *The art of coaching teams: Building resilient communities that transform schools.* San Francisco, CA: Wiley.

American Educator. (2003, Spring). The fourth-grade plunge: The cause; the cure. *American Educator* (Special issue).

American Psychiatric Association. (2013). *Diagnostic and statistical manual of mental disorders* (5th Ed.). Arlington, VA: Author.

Anderson, C. (2006). *The long tail: Why the future of business is selling less of more.* New York, NY: Hyperion.

Anderson, C. (2012). *Makers: The new industrial revolution.* New York, NY: Crown Business.

Baron-Cohen, S., & Klin, A. (2006). What's so special about Asperger syndrome? *Brain and Cognition, 61*(1), 1–4.

Barsalou, L. W. (1999a). Language comprehension: Archival memory or preparation for situated action. *Discourse Processes, 28,* 61–80.

Barsalou, L. W. (1999b). Perceptual symbol systems. *Behavioral and Brain Sciences, 22,* 577–660.

Barsalou, L. W. (2009). Simulation, situated conceptualization, and prediction. *Philosophical Transactions of the Royal Society B, 364,* 1281–1289.

Bazerman, C. (1989). *Shaping written knowledge.* Madison, WI: University of Wisconsin Press.

Beck, I. L., McKeown, M. G., & Kucan, L. (2002). *Bringing words to life: Robust vocabulary instruction.* New York, NY: Guilford Press.

Bereiter, C., & Scardamalia, M. (1993). *Surpassing ourselves: An inquiry into the nature and implications of expertise.* Chicago, IL: Open Court.

Bergen, B. K. (2012). *Louder than words: The new science of how the mind makes meaning.* New York, NY: Basic Books.

Biemiller, A. (2003). Oral comprehension sets the ceiling on reading comprehension. *American Educator, 27*(1), 23, 44.

Biskupic, J. (1995, May 10). Guns: A second (amendment) look. *Washington Post.*

Bizzell, P. (1992). *Academic discourse and critical consciousness.* Pittsburgh, PA: University of Pittsburgh Press.

Bransford, J. D., & Johnson, M. K. (1972). Contextual prerequisites for understanding: Some investigations of comprehension and recall. *Journal of Verbal Learning and Verbal Behavior, 11*(6), 717–726.

Brown, P., & Lauder, H. (2000). Collective intelligence. In S. Baron, J. Field, & T. Schuller (Eds.), *Social capital: Critical perspectives* (pp. 226–242). New York, NY: Oxford University Press.

Brown, S., & Vaughn, C. (2009). *Play: How it shapes the brain, opens the imagination, and invigorates the soul.* New York, NY: Penguin.

Buonomano, D. (2011). *Brain bugs: How the brain's flaws shape our lives.* New York, NY: W. W. Norton.

Carbaugh, D. (1996). *Situating selves: The communication of social identities in American scenes.* Albany, NY: State University of New York Press.

Center for the Developing Child at Harvard University. (2016). *From best practices to breakthrough impacts: A science-based approach to building a more promising future for young children and families.* Cambridge, MA: Harvard University. Retrieved from developingchild.harvard.edu

Chabris, C., & Simons, D. (2009). *The invisible gorilla: How our intuitions deceive us.* New York, NY: Crown.

Chi, M. T. H., Feltovich, P. J., & Glaser, R. (1981). Categorization and representation of physics problems by experts and novices. *Cognitive Science, 13*(2), 145–182.

Chomsky, N. (1986). *Knowledge of language: Its nature, origin, and use.* New York, NY: Praeger.

Clark, A. (1989). *Microcognition: Philosophy, cognitive science, and parallel distributed processing.* Cambridge, MA: MIT Press.

Clark, A. (1997). *Being there: Putting brain, body, and world together again.* Cambridge, MA: MIT Press.

Coates, J. M., & Herbert, J. (2008). Endogenous steroids and financial risk taking on a London trading floor. *Proceedings of the National Academy of Sciences, 105*(1), 6167–6172.

Cocker, M. (2001). *Birders: Tales of a tribe.* New York, NY: Atlantic Monthly Press.

Coren, M. J., & Fast Company. (2011, September 20). Foldit gamers solve riddle of HIV enzyme within 3 weeks. *Scientific American.* Retrieved from scientific-american.com/article/folditgamers-solve-riddle/

Cosmides, L. (1989). The logic of social exchange: Has natural selection shaped how humans reason? Studies with the Wasson Selection task. *Cognition, 31*(3), 187–276.

Cosmides, L., Barrett, H. C., & Tooby, J. (2010). Adaptive specializations, social exchange, and the evolution of human intelligence. *Proceedings of the National Academy of Sciences, 107,* 9007–9014.

Cosmides L., & Tooby, J. (2015). Adaptations for reasoning about social exchange. In D. M. Buss (Ed.), *The handbook of evolutionary psychology* (2nd ed.; vol. 2: *Integrations,* pp. 625–668). Hoboken, NJ: Wiley.

Csikszentmihályi, M. (1990). *Flow: The psychology of optimal experience.* New York, NY: Harper & Row.

Damasio, A. (1995). *Descartes' error: Emotion, reason, and the human brain.* New York, NY: Quill.

Damasio, A. (1999). *The feeling of what happens: Body and emotion in the making of consciousness.* Orlando, FL: Harvest Books.

Davidov, M., & Grusec, J. E. (2006). Untangling the links of parental responsiveness to distress and warmth to child outcomes. *Child Development, 77*(1), 44–58.

Dickinson, D. K. (1994). *Bridges to literacy: Children, families, and schools.* Cambridge, MA: Blackwell.

Dickinson, D. K., & Neuman, S. B. (Eds.). (2003). *Handbook of early literacy research: Volume 1.* New York, NY: Guilford Press.

Dickinson, D. K., & Neuman, S. B. (Eds.). (2006). *Handbook of early literacy research: Volume 2.* New York, NY: Guilford Press.

diSessa, A. A. (2000). *Changing minds: Computers, learning, and literacy.* Cambridge, MA: MIT Press.

Doherty-Sneddon, G., & Phelps, F. G. (2005). Gaze aversion: A response to cognitive or social difficulty? *Memory and Cognition, 3*(4), 727–733.

Doty, J. R. (2016). *Into the magic shop: A neurosurgeon's quest to discover the mysteries of the brain and the secrets of the heart.* New York, NY: Avery.

Duranti, A. (1992). *Linguistic anthropology.* Cambridge, MA: Cambridge University Press.

Eckert, P. (2008). Variation and the indexical field. *Journal of Sociolinguistics, 12*(4), 453–476.

Edelman, G. (1987). *Neural Darwinism: The theory of neuronal group selection.* New York, NY: Basic Books.

Eichenbaum, H. (2008). *Learning and memory.* New York, NY: Norton.

Elkind, D. (2007). *The power of play: Learning what comes naturally.* New York, NY: Da Capo Press.

Engeström, Y. (1987). *Learning by expanding: An activity theoretical approach to developmental research.* Helsinki, Finland: Orienta Konsultit.

Ericsson, K. A., & Kintsch, W. (1995). Long-term working memory. *Psychological Review, 102*(2), 211–245.

Erk, S., Kiefer, M., Grothe, J., Wunderlich, A. P., Spitzer, M., & Walter, H. (2003). Emotional context modulates subsequent memory effect. *Neuroimage, 18*(2), 439–447.

Fairclough, N. (Ed.). (1992). *Critical language awareness.* New York, NY: Taylor & Francis.

Ferguson, C. A. (1959). Diglossia. *Word, 15,* 325–340.

Ford, M. (2015). *The rise of the robots: Technology and the threat of a jobless future.* New York, NY: Basic Books.

Forster, E. M. (1927). *Aspects of the novel.* London, UK: Edward Arnold.

Gallese, V. (2007). Before and below "theory of mind": Embodied simulation and the neural correlates of social cognition. *Philosophical Transactions of the Royal Society B: Biological Sciences, 362,* 659–669.

Gallistel, R. R., & King, A. P. (2010). *Memory and the computational brain: Why cognitive science will transform neuroscience.* Malden, MA: Wiley-Blackwell.

Gardner-Neblett, N., & Gallagher, K. C. (2013). *More than baby talk: 10 ways to promote the language and communication skills of infants and toddlers.* Chapel Hill, NC: University of North Carolina, FPG Child Development Institute.

Gazzaniga, M. S. (1988). *Mind matters: How mind and brain interact to create our conscious lives*. Boston, MA: Houghton Mifflin.

Gazzaniga, M. (2011). *Who's in charge? Free will and the science of the brain*. New York, NY: HarperCollins.

Gee, J. P. (1994). First language acquisition as a guide for theories of learning and pedagogy. *Linguistics and Education, 6*(4), 331–354.

Gee, J. P. (2004). *Situated learning and language: A critique of traditional schooling*. London, UK: Routledge.

Gee, J. P. (2007). *What video games have to teach us about learning and literacy* (2nd ed.). New York, NY: Palgrave/Macmillan.

Gee, J. P. (2011). Reflections on empirical evidence on games and learning. In S. Tobias & J. D. Fletcher (Eds.), *Computer games and instruction* (pp. 223–232). Charlotte, NC: IAP.

Gee, J. P. (2013). *The anti-education era: Creating smarter students through digital media*. New York, NY: Palgrave/Macmillan.

Gee, J. P. (2014). *An introduction to discourse analysis: Theory and method* (4th ed.). London, UK: Routledge.

Gee, J. P. (2015a). *Literacy and education*. New York, NY: Routledge.

Gee, J. P. (2015b). *Social linguistics and literacies: Ideology in discourses* (5th ed.). London, UK: Taylor & Francis. (Original work published 1990)

Gee, J. P., & Hayes, E. R. (2010). *Women as gamers: The Sims and 21st century learning*. New York, NY: Palgrave.

Gee, J. P., & Hayes, E. R. (2011). *Language and learning in the digital age*. London, UK: Routledge.

Glenberg, A. M. (1997). What is memory for? *Behavioral and Brain Sciences, 20*(1), 1–55.

Glenberg, A. M., & Gallese, V. (2012). Action-based language: A theory of language acquisition, comprehension, and production. *Cortex, 48*(7), 905–922.

Godfrey-Smith, P. (2016). *Other minds: The octopus, the sea, and the deep origins of consciousness*. New York, NY: Farrar, Strauss, and Giroux.

Goffman, I. (1981). *Forms of talk*. Philadelphia, PA: University of Pennsylvania Press.

Goto, S. (2003). Basic writing and policy reform: Why we keep talking past each other. *Journal of Basic Writing, 21*(1), 16–32.

Graesser, A. C., Lu, S., Jackson, G. T., Mitchell, H., Ventura, M., Olney, A., & Louwerse, M. M. (2004). AutoTutor: A tutor with dialogue in natural language. *Behavior Research Methods, Instruments, and Computers, 36*(2), 180–193.

Gray, J. R., Braver, T. S., & Raichle, M. E. (2002). Integration of emotion and cognition in the lateral prefrontal cortex. *Proceedings of the National Academy of Sciences, 99*(6), 4115–4120.

Gumperz, J. J. (1982). *Discourse strategies*. Cambridge, UK: Cambridge University Press.

Hacking, I. (1985). Making up people. In T. C. Heller, M. Sosna, & D. E. Wellbery (Eds.), *Reconstructing individualism: Autonomy, individuality, and the self in Western thought* (pp. 222–236). Stanford, CA: Stanford University Press.

Hacking, I. (1994). The looping effects of human kinds. In D. Sperber, D. Premack, & A. J. Premack (Eds.), *Causal cognition: A multidisciplinary approach* (pp. 351–396). Oxford, UK: Clarendon Press.

Hacking, I. (2001). *The social construction of what*. Cambridge, MA: Harvard University Press.

Hall, E. T. (1976). *Beyond culture*. New York, NY: Anchor Books.

Halliday, M. A. K. (1978). *Language as social semiotics: The social interpretation of language and meaning*. London, UK: Edward Arnold.

Hanks, W. F. (1996). *Language and communicative practices*. Boulder, CO: Westview Press.

Hannaford, C. (2005). *Smart moves: Why learning is not all in your head* (2nd ed.). Salt Lake City, UT: Great River Books.

Harford, T. (2011). *Adapt: Why success always starts with failure*. New York, NY: Farrar, Straus, and Giroux.

Hart, T., & Risely, B. (1995). *Meaningful differences in the early experience of young American children*. Baltimore, MD: Brookes.

Hatch, M. (2014). *The maker-movement manifesto: Rules for innovation in the new world of crafters, hackers, and tinkerers*. New York, NY: McGraw-Hill.

Havelock, E. (1976). *Preface to Plato*. Cambridge, MA: Harvard University Press.

Hayes, E. R., & Gee, J. P. (2017, in press). Games as distributed teaching and learning systems. *Teachers College Record*.

Heath, S. B. (1983). *Ways with words: Language, life, and work in communities and classrooms*. Cambridge, UK: Cambridge University Press.

Hitt, J. (2013). *Bunch of amateurs: Inside America's hidden world of inventors, tinkerers, and job creators*. New York, NY: Broadway.

Holland, D., Lachicotte, W., Skinner, D., & Cain, C (1998). *Identity and agency in cultural worlds*. Cambridge, MA: Harvard University Press.

Holland, D., & Quinn, N. (Eds.). (1987). *Cultural models in language and thought*. Cambridge, UK: Cambridge University Press.

Holmes, J. (2016). Video games, informal teaching, and the rhetoric of design. Unpublished doctoral dissertation, Arizona State University, Tempe.

Hood, B. (2012). *The self illusion: How the social brain creates identity*. Oxford, UK: Oxford University Press.

Irvine, J. (2001). Style as distinctiveness: The culture and ideology of linguistic differentiation. In P. Eckert & J. Rickford (Eds.), *Style and sociolinguistic variation* (pp. 21–43). Cambridge, UK: Cambridge University Press.

Isenberg, N. (2016). *White trash: The 400-year untold history of class in America*. New York, NY: Viking.

Ito, M., Gutiérrez, K., Livingstone, S., Penuel, B., Rhodes, J., Salen, K., Schor, J., Sefton-Green, J., & Watkins, C. S. (2013). *Connected learning: An agenda for research and design*. Irvine, CA: Digital Media and Learning Hub.

James, W. (1884). What is an emotion? *Mind, 9*, 188–205.

Jenkins, H. (2006). *Convergence culture: Where old and new media collide*. New York, NY: NYU Press.

Junger, S. (2016). *Tribe: On homecoming and belonging*. New York, NY: Twelve.

Kahneman, D. (2011). *Thinking fast and slow*. New York, NY: Farrar, Straus, & Giroux.

Kendon, A. (1967). Some functions of gaze direction in social interaction. *Acta Psychologica, 26*(1), 22–63.

Kida, T. E. (2006). *Don't believe everything you think: The 6 basic mistakes we make in thinking*. Amherst, NY: Prometheus Books.

Kleck, R. E., & Strenta, A. (1980). Perceptions of the impact of negatively valued physical characteristics on social interaction. *Journal of Personality and Social Psychology, 39*(5), 861–873.

Klein, S. B., Robertson, T. E., & Delton A. W. (2010). Facing the future: Memory as an evolved system for planning future acts. *Memory and Cognition, 38*(1), 13–22.

Klein, S. B., Robertson, T. E., & Delton, A. W. (2011). The future-orientation of memory: Planning as a key component mediating the high levels of recall found with survival processing. *Memory, 19*(2), 121–139.

Krashen, S. D. (1982). *Principles and practice in second language acquisition.* Oxford, UK: Pergamon.

Labov, W. (1972). *Sociolinguistic patterns.* Philadelphia, PA: University of Pennsylvania Press.

Latour, B. (2005). *Reassembling the social: An introduction to actor-network-theory.* Oxford, UK: Oxford University Press.

Lavie, N., & Dalton, P. (2013). Load theory of attention and cognitive control. In S. Kastner & A. C. Nobre (Eds.), *Handbook of attention* (pp. 56–75). Oxford, UK: Oxford University Press.

Leadbeater, C., & Miller, P. (2004). *The Pro-Am revolution: How enthusiasts are changing our society and economy.* London, UK: Demos.

LeDoux, J. E. (1998). *The emotional brain: The mysterious underpinnings of emotional life.* New York, NY: Touchstone.

Leimeister, J. M. (2010). Collective intelligence. *Business and Information Systems Engineering, 4*(2), 245–248.

Lent, F. (2008). *The life of Saint Simeon Stylites: A translation of the Syriac text in Bedjan's Acta Martyrum et Sanctorum.* Pennsauken, NJ: Arx.

Levinas, E. (1969). *Totality and infinity.* Dordrecht, The Netherlands: Kluwer.

Levy, P. (1999). *Collective intelligence: Mankind's emerging world in cyberspace.* New York, NY: Basic Books.

Lewis, M. (2011). *The big short: Inside the doomsday machine.* New York, NY: Norton.

Loftus, E. (1976). *Memory: Surprising new insights into how we remember and how we forget.* Lanham, MD: Rowman & Littlefield.

Loftus, E., & Ketcham, K. (1991). *Witness for the defense: The accused, the eyewitness, and the expert who puts memory on trial.* New York, NY: St. Martin's Press.

Luntz, F. (2007). *Words that work: It's not what you say, it's what people hear.* New York, NY: Hachette.

Macknit, S. L., & Martinez-Conde, S. (2010). *Slights of mind: What the neuroscience of magic reveals about our everyday deceptions.* New York, NY: Henry Holt.

Malone, T. (2004). *The future of work: How the new order of business will shape your organization, your management style, and your life.* Cambridge, MA: Harvard Business Review Press.

Maloneya, M. T., & Mulherin, J. H. (2003). The complexity of price discovery in an efficient market: The stock market reaction to the Challenger crash. *Journal of Corporate Finance, 9*(4), 453–479.

Marcus, G. (2008). *Kluge: The haphazard evolution of the human mind.* New York, NY: Houghton Mifflin.

Marcus, G., & Freeman, J. (Eds.). (2015). *The future of the brain: Essays by the world's leading neuroscientists.* Princeton, NJ: Princeton University Press.

Margolis, H. (1987). *Patterns, thinking, and cognition: A theory of judgment.* Chicago, IL: University of Chicago Press.

Marmot, M. (2004). *The status syndrome: How social standing affects our health and longevity.* New York, NY: Holt.

Martin, E. (2007). *Bipolar expeditions: Mania and depression in American culture.* Princeton, NJ: Princeton University Press.

Mayer, E. (2016). *The mind-gut connection: How the hidden conversation within our bodies impacts our mood, our choices, and our overall health.* New York, NY: Harper Wave.

McAuliffe, K. (2016). *This is your brain on parasites: How tiny creatures manipulate our behavior and shape society.* Boston, MA: Houghton Mifflin Harcourt.

McGaugh, J. L., Cahill, L., & Roozendaal, B. (1996). Involvement of the amygdala in memory storage: Interactions with other brain systems. *Proceedings of the National Academy of Sciences, 93*(24), 1350–1351.

Mehler, L., & Bever, T. G. (1967). Cognitive capacity of very young children. *Science, 158*(3797), 141–142.

Michaels, S. (1981). "Sharing time": Children's narrative styles and differential access to literacy. *Language in Society, 10*(3), 423–442.

Miller, J. D., & Inglehart, R. (2012). American attitudes toward science and technology. In W. S. Bainbridge (Ed.), *Leadership in science and technology: A reference handbook* (Vol. 1, pp. 298–306). New York, NY: Sage.

Milroy, L. (1991). *Language and social networks* (2nd ed.). Oxford, UK: Blackwell.

Moss, M. (2013). *Salt, sugar, fat: How the food giants hooked us.* New York, NY: Random House.

Nerbribk, E., & Borch, E. (1993). Evaluation of bacterial contamination at separate processing stages in emulsion sausage production. *International Journal of Food Microbiology, 20*(1), 37–44.

Neuman, S. B., & Celano, D. C. (2012). *Giving our children a fighting chance: Poverty, literacy, and the development of information capital.* New York, NY: Teachers College Press.

New London Group. (1996). A pedagogy of multiliteracies: Designing social futures. *Harvard Education Review, 66*(1), 60–92.

Newton-Small, J. (2016). *Broad influence: How women are changing the way America works.* New York, NY: Time Books.

Nielsen, M. (2012). *Reinventing discovery: The new era of networked science.* Princeton, NJ: Princeton University Press.

Obermaier, F., & Obermayer, B. (2016). *The Panama Papers: Breaking the story of how the rich and powerful hide their money.* London, UK: Oneworld.

Ochs, E., Gonzales, P., & Jacoby, S. (1996). "When I come down I'm in a domain state": Talk, gesture, and graphic representation in the interpretive activity of physicists. In E. Ochs, E. Schegloff, & S. Thompson (Eds.), *Interaction and grammar* (pp. 329–369). Cambridge, UK: Cambridge University Press.

Ochs, E., Shohet, M., Campos, B., & Beck, M. (2010). "Coming together at dinner": A study of working families. In K. Cjrostemsem & B. Schneider (Eds.), *Workplace flexibility: Realigning 20th-century jobs for a 21st-century workforce* (pp. 57–70). Ithaca, NY: Cornell University Press.

Olson, D. R. (1977). From utterance to text: The bias of language in speech and writing. *Harvard Education Review, 47*(3), 257–281.

Olson, D. R. (1996). *The world on paper: The conceptual and cognitive implications of writing and reading.* Cambridge, UK: Cambridge University Press.

Ong, W. (1982). *Orality and literacy: The technologizing of the word.* London, UK: Methuen.

Orenstein, P. (2016). *Girls and sex: Navigating the complicated new landscape.* New York, NY: HarperCollins.

Padden, C. A., & Humphries, T. L. (2005). *Inside deaf culture.* Cambridge, MA: Harvard University Press.

Parker, G. (2002). *Cross-functional teams: Working with allies, enemies, and other strangers.* San Francisco, CA: Jossey-Bass.

Piaget, J. (1965). *The child's conception of number.* New York, NY: Norton.

Pickett, K., & Wilkinson, R. (2011). *The spirit level: Why greater equality makes societies stronger.* New York, NY: Bloomsbury.

Pinker, S. (1994). *The language instinct: How the mind creates language.* New York, NY: William Marrow.

Pollak, S. D., Vardi, S., Putzer Bechner, A. M., & Curtin, J. J. (2005). Physically abused children's regulation of attention in response to hostility. *Child Development, 76*(5), 968–977.

Popper, K. R. (1994). *The myth of the framework: In defense of science and rationality.* London, UK: Routledge.

Quine, W. V. O. (1951). Two dogmas of empiricism. *The Philosophical Review, 60*(1), 20–43.

Reed, W. J. (2001). The Pareto, Zipf, and other power laws. *Economic Letters, 74*(1), 15–19.

Reeves, B., & Nass, C. (1999). *The media equation: How people treat computers, television, and new media like real people and places.* New York, NY: Cambridge University Press.

Reich, R. B. (1992). *The work of nations.* New York, NY: Vintage Books.

Reich, R. B. (2010). *Aftershock: The next economy and America's future.* New York, NY: Vintage.

Renfrew, C. (2009). *Prehistory: The making of the human mind.* New York, NY: Random House.

Rhyner, P. M. (Ed.). (2009). *Emergent literacy and language development: Promoting learning in early childhood.* New York, NY: Guilford.

Richards, J. M., & Gross, J. J. (2000). Emotion regulation and memory: The cognitive costs of keeping one's cool. *Journal of Personality and Social Psychology, 79*(3), 410–424.

Rose, S. A., & Blank, M. (1974). The potency of context in children's cognition: An illustration through conservation. *Child Development, 45*(2), 499–502.

Rosenblatt, L. (2005). *Making meaning with texts: Selected essays.* Portsmouth, NH: Heinemann.

Sacks, H., & Schegloff, E. (1974). A simplest systematics for the organization of turn-taking for conversation. *Language, 50*(4), 696–735.

Sales, N. J. (2016). *American girls: Social media and the secret lives of teenagers.* New York, NY: Knopf.

Schacter, D. L. (2002). *The seven sins of memory: How the mind forgets and remembers.* New York, NY: Houghton Mifflin.

Schiffrin, D. (1987). *Discourse markers*. Cambridge, UK: Cambridge University Press.

Schleppegrell, M. (2004). *Language of schooling: A functional linguistics perspective*. Mahwah, NJ: Lawrence Erlbaum.

Schön, D. A. (1983). *The reflective practitioner: How professionals think in action*. New York, NY: Basic Books

Schwartz, D. L., & Arena D. (2013). *Measuring what matters most: Choice-based assessments for the digital age*. Cambridge, MA: MIT Press.

Scollon, R., & Scollon, S. W. (1981). *Narrative, literacy, and face in interethnic communication*. Norwood, NJ: Ablex.

Shaffer, D. W. (2007). *How computer games help children learn*. New York, NY: Palgrave Macmillan.

Shirky, C. (2008). *Here comes everybody: The power of organizing without organizations*. New York, NY: Penguin.

Shirky, C. (2010). *Cognitive surplus: Creativity and generosity in a connected age*. New York, NY: Penguin.

Simons, D. J., & Chabris, C. F. (2011). What people believe about how memory works: A representative survey of the U.S. population. *PLoS ONE, 6*(8), e22757.

Snow, C. E. (1986). Conversations with children. In P. Fletcher & M. Garman (Eds.), *Language acquisition* (2nd ed., pp. 69–89). Cambridge, UK: Cambridge University Press.

Snow, C. E. (1991). The theoretical basis for relationships between language and literacy in development. *Journal of Research in Childhood Education, 6*(1), 5–10.

Snow, C. E., Burns, M. S., & Griffin, P. (Eds.). (1998). *Preventing reading difficulties in young children*. Washington, DC: National Academy Press.

Sorkin, A. R. (2009). *Too big to fail: The inside story of how Wall Street and Washington fought to save the financial system—and themselves*. London, UK: Viking Penguin.

Soroush, A. (2000). *Reason, freedom, and democracy in Islam: Essential writings of Abdolkarim Soroush*. Oxford, UK: Oxford University Press.

Stanovich, K. E. (2000). *Progress in understanding reading: Scientific foundations and new frontiers*. New York, NY: Guilford Press.

Steinkuehler, C., Compton-Lilly, C., & King, E. (2010). Reading in the context of online games. In K. Gomez, L. Lyons, & J. Radinsky (Eds.), *Learning in the disciplines: Proceedings of the 9th International Conference of the Learning Sciences (ICLS 2010), Volume 1, Full Papers* (pp. 222–230). Chicago, IL: International Society of the Learning Science.

Stiglitz, J. E. (2013). *The price of inequality: How today's divided society endangers our future*. New York, NY: Norton.

Strauss, C., & Quinn, N. (1997). *A cognitive theory of cultural meaning*. Cambridge, UK: Cambridge University Press.

Sunstein, C. R., & Hastie, R. (2015). *Wiser: Getting beyond groupthink to make groups smarter*. Cambridge, MA: Harvard Business Review Press.

Surowiecki, J. (2004). *The wisdom of crowds: Why the many are smarter than the few and how collective wisdom shapes business, economies, societies, and nations*. New York, NY: Doubleday.

Swaab, D. F. (2014). *We are our brains: A neurobiography of the brain from the womb to Alzheimer's*. New York, NY: Spiegel & Grau.

Taleb, N. N. (2006). *The black swan: The impact of the highly improbable.* New York, NY: Random House.

Taleb, N. N. (2012). *Antifragile: Things that gain from disorder.* New York, NY: Random House.

Tomasello, M. (2014). *A natural history of human thinking.* Cambridge, MA: Harvard University Press.

Tough, P. (2012). *How children succeed: Grit, curiosity, and the hidden power of character.* New York, NY: Houghton Mifflin Harcourt.

Vygotsky, L. S. (1978). *Mind in society: The development of higher psychological processes.* Cambridge, MA: Harvard University Press.

Waldman, M. (2014). *The second amendment: A biography.* New York, NY: Simon & Schuster.

Wallach, W. (2015). *Master: How to keep technology from slipping beyond our control.* New York, NY: Basic Books.

Warner, M. (2013). *Pandora's lunchbox: How processed food took over the American meal.* New York, NY: Scribner.

Wason, P. (1966). Reasoning. In B. M. Foss (Ed.), *New horizons in psychology* (pp. 135–151). Harmondsworth, UK: Penguin.

Wason, P. (1968). Reasoning about a rule. *Quarterly Journal of Experimental Psychology, 20*(3), 273–281.

Weinberger, D. (2012). *Too big to know: Rethinking knowledge now that the facts aren't the facts, experts are everywhere, and the smartest person in the room is the room.* New York, NY: Basic Books.

Wertsch, J. V. (1985). *Vygotsky and the social formation of mind.* Cambridge, MA: Harvard University Press.

Wieder, D. L., & Pratt, S. (1990). On being a recognizable Indian among Indians. In D. Carbaugh (Ed.), *Cultural communication and intercultural contact* (pp. 45–64). Hillsdale, NJ: Erlbaum.

Williams, R. (1983). *The year 2000.* New York, NY: Pantheon Books.

Wilson, M. (2002). Six views of embodied cognition. *Psychonomic Bulletin and Review, 9*(4), 625–636.

Wohlson, M. (2011). *Biopunk: How DIY scientists hack the software of life.* New York, NY: Penguin.

Woolley, A., & Malone, T. (2011). Defend your research: What makes a team smarter? More women. *Harvard Business Review, 89*(6), 32–33.

Yong, E. (2016). *I contain multitudes: The microbes within us and a grander view of life.* New York, NY: HarperCollins.

Younge, G. (2016). *Another day in the death of America: A chronicle of ten short lives.* New York, NY: Nation Books.

Zolli, A., & Healy, A. M. (2012). *Resilience: Why things bounce back.* New York, NY: Simon & Schuster.

Index

About the Author

James Paul Gee, Mary Lou Fulton Presidential Professor of Literacy Studies and Regents' Professor at Arizona State University, is a fellow of the American Educational Research Association and a member of the National Academy of Education.

Printed and bound by CPI Group (UK) Ltd, Croydon, CR0 4YY

13/04/2025

14656614-0001